A SHORT HISTORY
of THOMISM

ROMANUS CESSARIO, O.P.

A SHORT HISTORY
of THOMISM

The Catholic University of America Press
Washington, D.C.

International Copyright © 2003

Editoriale Jaca Book Spa, Milan

All rights reserved

Published in Italian with the original title: IL TOMISMO E I TOMISTI

within the series *Per una Storia d'Occidente. Chiesa e Società* ed.

Guy Bedouelle, Editoriale Jaca Book Spa, Milan, Italy.

U.S.A. edition published by arrangement with

Eulama Literary Agency, Rome.

Copyright © 2005

The Catholic University of America Press

All rights reserved

LIBRARY OF CONGRESS CATALOGING-IN-PUBLICATION DATA

Cessario, Romanus.

[Tomismoe e i tomisti. English]

A short history of Thomism / Romanus Cessario.

p.   cm.

Includes bibliographical references and index.

ISBN 0-8132-1386-x (pbk. : alk. paper)

1. Thomas, Aquinas, Saint, 1225?–1274. I. Title.

B765.T54C4613 2005

149´.91—dc22

2004002866

For

JOHN AQUINAS FARREN, O.P.

Rector, Saint John's Seminary

&

Sometime Director of the Leonine Commission

Contents

Foreword

That brevity is the soul of wit may seem an ironic remark when we consider its connection with Polonius, but it contains an important, one might almost say Thomistic, truth. Simplicity in an important sense rides on profundity. It is the mark of the wise man that he can marshal and order vast amounts of material, and possesses a keen sense of the beginning, the middle, and the end of inquiry; only a very learned author could have provided the *tour du monde thomiste* that Father Romanus Cessario gives us here. Thomas Aquinas himself was not much given to historical surveys, save for those he found in the Aristotelian treatises on which he commented, but Cessario may be said to mimic his master in that he has written a survey of the history of Thomism which will be read with ease by the beginner and with delight and admiration by those who have spent a lifetime with the text of Aquinas.

What is a Thomist? What is Thomism? In the introductory part, Cessario puts before the reader, with a marvelous ease of erudition his footnotes can only suggest, the ways these questions have been understood and answered. Out of the discussion emerges his own suggestion: he will write a *histoire fleuve* of the school as he has defined it that emphasizes the unity of some seven hundred and more years, noting without overstating the influence of historical events and the shifting geographical centers of gravity of Thomism. The result will enable the reader to navigate those centuries under the captaincy of an author who has a compass in hand and an eye for the far horizon.

We are often rightly told that Thomas was principally a theologian, but the reminder has sometimes been made in order to downplay the importance of Thomas as a philosopher. Cessario reminds us that Thomas as theologian has given us the most formal distinction between theology and philosophy, a distinction that enables us to identify philosophical discourse when we see it, in Thomas and elsewhere, but which does not preclude the role that philosophy plays within theology. Cessario emphasizes the unity of theology for Thomas and gently chides those who would fragment sacred doctrine into a number of constituent specialties. The subject of theology is God himself and the viewpoint is the sapiential one vouchsafed us by revelation.

For all that, philosophy has its own integrity for Thomas, and it is no accident that so many of the great Thomists of the twentieth century were philosophers, and indeed laymen. Philosophy remains the *lingua franca* enabling believers and non-believers to come together in the recognition of naturally knowable truths. The resulting wisdom can seem exiguous to the believer, and it is, but it manifests the range of reason and the natural truths presupposed by theology and put to a higher purpose.

Father Cessario enables us to see the long and checkered history of Thomism, and he brings us into the present where temptations to prophesy and predict present themselves. Whither Thomism? The long and unbroken patronage of the teaching Church has proven a stimulus to generations of students of Thomas. In these latter times, it is often suggested that Thomism lost its hegemony at Vatican II, and that efforts to revive it are counter-revolutionary. Perhaps. But as Cessario enables us to see, the supposed corpse did not show up for its funeral. Moreover, there seems to be afoot a new flourishing of Thomism, however we characterize those thinkers who find inspiration in Thomas's writings. It is not the label that is important, finally, nor indeed the man. Leo XIII wrote that we find more in Thomas than Thomas himself. Indeed. And that more is a truth that transcends personal ownership. Thomism in the public domain is a good thing since, in philosophy at least, the thought of Thomas is grounded in what everybody knows. This wise little book will doubtless play a role in that flourishing.

Ralph McInerny
University of Notre Dame

A SHORT HISTORY
of THOMISM

Chapter One

THOMISM

In the broadest sense of the term, "Thomism" refers to a body of tenets in both philosophy and theology that derive from and are held to represent faithfully the doctrine of the thirteenth-century Italian priest Thomas Aquinas (1224/5–1274). But Thomism stands for more than an accumulation of teachings: it also embodies a conception of philosophical and theological enquiry that owes its genius to the insight and resourcefulness of the first Thomist. In his 1988 Gifford Lectures, Alasdair MacIntyre carefully demonstrates that Aquinas's approach to theology provides a standpoint that suffers from less incoherence, is more comprehensive and more resourceful, especially in its ability to deal calmly, critically, and yet creatively with opposing views, than that espoused, for instance, by an encyclopedist, who imposes on knowledge a single framework, albeit one designed to keep truth up-to-date with progress, or a genealogist, who asserts, together with Friedrich Nietzsche (d. 1900), that all knowledge leads to a multiplicity of perspectives, each with its own claim to truth-from-a-point-of-view.[1] Since the last quarter of the thirteenth century, Thomists have, at various times and in different places, defended, disputed, and even developed one or another of the teachings of Thomas Aquinas. At the same time, those most worthy of the name have striven to imitate their master's profound understanding of, and deep respect for, what MacIntyre calls the "rationality of tradition."

Aquinas's prominence in the intellectual history of the West originates above all in the value that the Roman Catholic Church has attached to his intellectual accomplishments. Recognized by the Church as one of her official teachers or doctors, Thomas Aquinas united an uncommonly comprehensive knowledge of theology with a sharply disciplined philosophical mind. Furthermore, both his own religious consecration and the personal appropriation of Gospel values that it symbolizes helped this Dominican friar realize with special clarity the vocation to serve as a teacher of truth. The universal compass of his scholarly achievements explains the custom whereby the Church even today venerates Thomas Aquinas as her "Common Doctor," a title that confirms the pervasiveness of his influence, at least in the West, on the received theology and philosophy that is practiced in Christian schools and used to illuminate authentic Church teaching.

I. WHO IS THOMAS AQUINAS?

Thomas Aquinas was born to a landed aristocratic family that played a conspicuous role in the turbulent political life of the early thirteenth-century Italian peninsula. But unlike Augustine of Hip-

---

1. See his *Three Rival Versions of Moral Enquiry* (Notre Dame, Ind.: University of Notre Dame Press, 1990).

po, also a foundational doctor from the Western Church, Thomas d'Aquino, notwithstanding his prolific writing, surrenders very few details of his own biography, and so our knowledge of his family interactions and other personal matters are few and almost all secondhand, mostly from Aquinas's hagiographers. Even though we must rely on other sources to compose Aquinas's biographical sketch, the saint's theological and philosophical compositions nonetheless disclose both his own spirit as a Christian believer and the magnitude of his intellectual acumen. The French scholar Jean-Pierre Torrell supplies the most recent biographical and bibliographical information in his two important volumes, *Saint Thomas Aquinas*, vol. 1, *The Person and His Work*, vol. 2, *Spiritual Master*.[2]

Thomas Aquinas was born and spent his early years in the Kingdom of Sicily. It was a time when Frederick II (1194–1250) and Pope Gregory IX (c. 1148–1241) were at warring odds with one another, and in 1239, when Aquinas was fourteen, the pope excommunicated Frederick, since by that time he had initiated an invasion into the States of the Church as part of a long-delayed offensive against the Lombard communes. This historically noteworthy clash between civil and ecclesiastical authority was only the first of many conflicts that would dominate the societal circumstances in which Thomas Aquinas constructed his massive corpus of theological and philosophical writings. Later at Paris, new conflicts on the one hand between diocesan clergy and religious orders and on the other between Aristotelian philosophers and Augustinian theologians again provided both background and stimulus for Aquinas's intellectual work. And later still in Italy, long-standing

2. Washington, D.C.: The Catholic University of America, 1996, 2003.

antagonisms, embodied in a then two-hundred-year-old schism, between the See of Rome and the Churches of the East dictated, in large measure, the way in which Aquinas would deploy his intellectual energies. Even toward the end of his life, Aquinas was compelled to confront conflictual circumstances, but this time in the form of intramural squabbles between his fellow Dominicans, some of whom still considered that ordained ministry could best be learned after the fashion of a guild-craft, while others, inspired by Aquinas's own example, appreciated that the Christian priest, because he participates in Christ's own mediation, requires a scientific instruction in the deposit of saving Truth.

Conflicts such as those that overshadowed Aquinas's personal background resulted, for the most part, from the growth and strengthening of centralizing tendencies in both ecclesiastical and secular affairs that took place at the beginning of the thirteenth century. The unprecedented expression of political as well as theological unity in the Church achieved by Pope Innocent III at the Fourth Lateran Council in 1215 inaugurates this period of profound cultural change, which made an impact even on Aquinas's treatment of speculative concepts like natural law.[3] In order to appreciate fully the kind of stability that Aquinas's theology and philosophical investigations introduced into the world of Catholic thought, one must recall the turbulence that marked the social, political, and ecclesiastical milieus in the first half of the thirteenth century.

The intellectual stimulation that characterizes the high period of scholastic schoolmen grew out of what M.-D. Chenu has forth-

---

3. See Alasdair MacIntyre, "Natural Law as Subversive: The Case of Aquinas," *Journal of Medieval and Early Modern Studies* 26 (1996): 61–83.

rightly described as the renaissance of the twelfth century.[4] The social changes and other forms of human development occasioned by the transition from feudal to urban Europe formed the background for the scholastic revival of the thirteenth century. Chenu's claim represented a challenge to the prevailing views then held by most mid-nineteenth-century historians, especially German scholars such as Burckhardt and Voigt, who were accustomed to portray European culture before the renaissance of the sixteenth century as darkly glum. Keenly aware of the anti-medieval bias at work in such representations, Chenu instead took inspiration from the nineteenth-century French historian J.-J.-A. Ampère, who had successfully shown in his *Histoire littéraire de la France avant le douzième siècle* that Christian civilization in the West underwent at least two extraordinary renaissances before the humanist reawakening in the sixteenth century. It was, in fact, the twelfth-century renaissance, when a massive effort was mounted to retrieve and organize past learning in many fields, that enabled Aquinas to make creative use of the many philosophical advances that accompanied the introduction of Aristotle into the West.[5]

Educated first with the Benedictine monks at Monte Cassino and later in Naples at the first European university to operate under entirely secular control—which Frederick II founded in 1224—the young Thomas Aquinas enjoyed the usual prerogatives associated with his social class and standing. It is commonly assumed, moreover, that the cadet son of Landolfo and Theodora d'Aquino

4. "Nature and Man: The Renaissance of the Twelfth Century," chap. 1, *La théologie au douzième siècle* (Paris: Vrin, 1957).

5. F. Van Steenberghen, *Aristotle in the West: The Origins of Latin Aristotelianism,* 2nd ed., trans. Leonard Johnson (Louvain: Nauwelaerts, 1970).

was destined to pursue an ecclesiastical career of distinction. However, the direction of his life changed dramatically when he abandoned the aspirations that were those of his family, especially of his mother, and joined the newly established international brotherhood of Dominicans. The traditional accounts of his attempt to join the friars, which include tales of imprisonment and attempted seduction, reveal the emotional conflict that Aquinas's decision created within his own family.

Studies in Paris and Cologne followed. In these centers of intellectual life, Aquinas joined other young Dominicans who had been placed under the tutelage of Albertus Magnus, the early Dominican theologian and natural scientist whose life and works Simon Tugwell describes as holy and brilliant respectively.[6] By following the prescribed lectures of the curriculum, Aquinas prepared himself to assume a university teaching post in Paris. His education was not only traditional, involving close studies of the Scriptures, of the Western Fathers, and of Church law, but also innovative inasmuch as Aquinas discovered the new wave of Aristotelian philosophy, which included the areas of natural, moral, and rational (rhetoric, grammar, and logic) philosophy. This estimate is based on Fernand Van Steenberghen's reconstruction of the standard curriculum in place at the University of Paris toward 1240.[7] Between 1252 and 1259, Aquinas fulfilled with signal success the obligations of a thirteenth-century university instructor and professor, notwithstanding the conflicts and disputes that continued both within and outside of the lecture halls. Rapid developments that

6. See his "Introduction," *Albert and Thomas: Selected Writings* (New York: Paulist Press, 1988), pp. 3–39 and 96–116.

7. *La Philosophie au XIIIe Siècle* (Louvain: Éditions Peeters, 1991), pp. 109–22.

were then taking place in the field of theology obliged Aquinas to hone further his critical abilities, and he became adept at navigating the intellectually challenging waters of the medieval scholastic *disputatio.* On 15 August 1257, both he and the Franciscan doctor Bonaventure were admitted to the *consortium magistrorum* (teachers' association).

Between 1259 and 1268, Aquinas again resided on the Italian peninsula, where he accomplished a variety of tasks in service to both the papacy and the Dominican Order. The earlier portions of one of his better known works, the *Summa theologiae,* date from this period. His *Summa* was developed as an effort, exerted on behalf of Dominican students in Rome, to make divine revelation intelligible after the fashion of a scientific body of truths ordered around a single principle. Circumstances of conflict, however, once more directed the course of Aquinas's apostolic activity, bringing him back to Paris for a second period of teaching between 1268 and 1272. Once arrived again in the City of Lights, he devoted his energies to allaying the uneasiness that the pagan philosophy of Aristotle caused among theologians of a more traditional Augustinian persuasion, while at the same time he critically engaged those who used philosophy to contradict the truths of the Catholic faith. In the meantime, Aquinas continued an earlier battle in defense of the mendicant religious orders, such as the Franciscans and Dominicans, whose newly authorized place within the University structure created certain tensions among the already-established secular masters. After the three-year cycle of lectures and disputations that constituted a term of office for the Dominican chair at the University of Paris, Thomas Aquinas returned once again to his native land and place of religious assignation. At Naples, he took up his academic work, teaching Dominicans about the Bible and continuing to write his *Summa theologiae*.

During his first sojourn in the Papal States, Aquinas had, among other intellectual accomplishments, composed a compendium of arguments to be used by the papal theologians charged with carrying on dialogue with Byzantine theologians. So when Pope Gregory X convoked a council at Lyons for 1 May 1274, he numbered Thomas among the experts who were asked to join the deliberations, since the purpose of this council was to achieve mutual understanding with the separated Greeks. However, while traveling northward from Naples, Aquinas suffered a sudden decline in his health, and on Wednesday, 7 March, he died in the early hours of the morning at the Cistercian monastery of Fossanova. Dead at 49 years of age, Thomas Aquinas nonetheless left a significant corpus of works on Scripture, philosophy, and theology, as well as producing other learned writings both practical and speculative.

The nineteenth-century printed editions of Aquinas's works contain between 25 (Parma, 1852–73) and 34 (Vivès, 1871–72) volumes, whereas the first complete edition, edited by Jesuit Father Roberto Busa with the aid of computer technology, contains seven volumes (Stuttgart–Bad Cannstatt, 1980). Faithful to his ideals of mendicant simplicity and to fulfilling the Dominican objective of preaching sacred truth, Aquinas, during the course of his adult life, politely avoided becoming both the abbot of Monte Cassino and the archbishop of Naples, the former at the start of his career, and the latter at its end. By these decisions, he disengaged himself from the arenas of weighty but nonetheless parochial conflicts, and so was free to make a permanent contribution to theological learning in the universal Church.

Thomas Aquinas proceeded on the supposition that all theological writing ought to reflect the unity of divine truth: in his phrase, "like an imprint on us of God's own knowledge, which is single and simple vision of everything."[8] For Aquinas, then, the discipline of theology does not emerge out of a constellation of diverse fields of scientific inquiry that are marshaled into Christian service. Rather, as a single divine science about God, theology embraces each of the subordinate and ancillary disciplines within its transcendental unity and so is able to express the one divine knowledge that governs without qualification everything that exists. In other words, Aquinas was persuaded that the best theology reflects the simplicity of God whose knowledge of himself remains the one source of all true wisdom. Consequently, it is not easy to break down Aquinas's works to fit the modern categories that theologians use to classify and describe their work; indeed, it would have struck him as very odd to witness the modern penchant for dividing theology up into different fields of enquiry. On the contrary, Aquinas was tremendously taken by the fact that only the theologian enjoys the prerogative of grasping the unity of truth that flows from the divine simplicity, and so would have been repelled by the cacophony of competing truth claims advanced by point-of-view theologians claiming hegemonic expertise in one or another theological discipline. At the same time, because Aquinas understood that theology is about ordering truths to the one Truth, and not assembling facts about many different topics, none of Aquinas's works fits the literary genre of the encyclopedia, which

8. *Summa theologiae* Ia, q. 1, a. 3, ad 2: "velut quaedam impressio divinae scientiae, quae est una et simplex omnium."

always depends on recent research to modify what until then had been provisionally considered as true. In sum, Aquinas recognized the formal difference that distinguishes theology as a divine science from philosophy, which always remains bound by the limits that human reason imposes.

A particular conception of the unity of theology did not keep Aquinas from developing an interest in the various fields that are related to theological inquiry. During his relatively brief professional career between 1252 (omitting his earlier expositions of certain Old Testament books, *viz.,* Isaiah, Jeremiah, and Lamentations, which he composed as a young student while in Cologne with Albertus Magnus) and 1273, when he stopped writing altogether after undergoing on 6 December a profoundly religious experience while praying in the chapel of Saint Nicholas in the Dominican Church at Naples, Aquinas produced theological literature that fits every description: theological syntheses, disputed questions, biblical commentaries, commentaries on Aristotle, commentaries on other classical works commonly in use at medieval universities, polemical writings, treatises on specific subjects, letters and requests for expert opinions on particular issues, liturgical works, sermons, and prayers. Gilles Emery provides the full titles of Aquinas's works in "A Brief Catalogue of the Works of Saint Thomas Aquinas,"[9] which brings up to date the list established by J. A. Weisheipl,[10] following that of I. T. Eschmann, "A Catalogue of St. Thomas's Works."[11] All in all, a rich array of publications for

9. Torrell, *Saint Thomas Aquinas,* vol. 1, pp. 330–61.

10. *Friar Thomas d'Aquino: His Life, Thought, and Work* (New York: Doubleday, 1974), with Corrigenda and Addenda (Washington, D.C.: The Catholic University of America Press, 1983), pp. 355–405.

11. E. Gilson, *The Christian Philosophy of St. Thomas Aquinas,* trans. L. K. Shook (New York: Random House, 1956), pp. 381–437.

one thirteenth-century man to produce within a period of little over twenty years, even taking into account the fact that he was at times aided by as many as four secretaries.

It may be useful to observe at this point that certain works of Aquinas influenced more profoundly the subsequent Thomist tradition than did others. Among the most influential, the theological syntheses stand out: The *Scriptum super libros Sententiarum,* a commentary on the four books of Peter Lombard's *Sentences;* the *Summa contra gentiles,* a systematic account of the main doctrines of the Christian religion; and especially, the *Summa theologiae,* begun after Aquinas had decided not to revise his writings on the *Sentences,* and undoubtedly the work for which he is best known as a theologian. The first of these, Aquinas's *Sentences,* as they are sometimes called, were very influential in the centuries immediately following his death, whereas the two *summae* began to dominate the Thomist tradition sometime before the sixteenth century. In recent years, experts have pointed out that in order to grasp the full breadth of Aquinas's learning, it is required to study the entirety of Aquinas's *corpus,* especially his commentaries on the Sacred Scriptures and on Aristotle.

2. SPEAKING ABOUT THOMISM

Although the epithet "Thomist" has been used since the fourteenth century to identify those who subscribe to the principles of Thomism, scholars still debate the best way to identify the movement. For example, Géry Prouvost prefers to underline the discontinuities among those who have read and commented upon Aquinas.[12] Citing theoretical issues such as the relation of philoso-

12. *Thomas d'Aquin et les thomismes* (Paris: Le Cerf, 1996).

phy to theology, the question of "l'être," and the status of our knowledge of God, Prouvost chooses to emphasize the divergences among Thomists: "Over the course of history, almost every thesis essential to Thomas was either contested or ignored by one or another of the 'Thomists.'"[13] He has advanced, moreover, the striking hypothesis that, on account of its own internal evolution, Thomism, at least in its traditional scholastic form, disappeared from the stage of secular thought after the "moment cartésien," and, from the start of the 1950s, no longer could be counted among the active theological traditions at work in the Church. While Prouvost admittedly points up the complexities involved in sketching a history of Thomism, his deconstructionist construal of that history is not widely shared. Indeed, ongoing research in Aquinas carried on by theologians and philosophers and the sustained interest that scholars therefore still give to the Thomist commentatorial tradition make it difficult to accept the suggestion that Thomism is dead.[14] On the contrary, there are solid grounds to maintain the view that at the start of the twenty-first century, Thomism remains an active intellectual tradition in both secular and religious circles.

One sign of the vitality of Thomism remains the serious and detailed attention to its history and teachings that the standard reference books continue to provide in the form of articles on both the general topic of Thomism and the principal figures in its history. For example, a few decades after the nineteenth-century revival

13. Ibid., p. 9: "à peu près toutes les thèses essentielles de Thomas furent, au cours de l'histoire, soit contestées, soit ignorées par l'un ou l'autre 'thomiste.'"

14. For example, see Jean-Pierre Torrell, "Situation actuelle des études thomistes," *Recherches de Science Religieuse* 91 (2003): 343–71.

of Thomism had begun in Europe, the American Dominican D. J. Kennedy, who had been trained in Europe and taught briefly at the University of Fribourg in Switzerland, gave this definition of the school to which he belonged: "In a broad sense, Thomism is the name given to the system which follows the teaching of St. Thomas Aquinas in philosophical and theological questions. In a restricted sense, the term is applied to a group of opinions held by a school called Thomistic, composed principally, but not exclusively, of members of the Order of St. Dominic, these same opinions being attacked by other philosophers or theologians, many of whom profess to be followers of St. Thomas."[15] While Kennedy sharpens the contrasts among Thomists, and even suggests something of the pugnacity that frequently attended the development of Thomism, this early American Thomist correctly pointed out a perennial truth for understanding the parameters of Thomism: not everyone who studies and even cites the texts of Aquinas qualifies as a bonafide Thomist.

Writing in the mid-twentieth century, J. A. Weisheipl, who benefitted from and later contributed to the large-scale historical and systematic studies in medieval philosophy and theology that Étienne Gilson had begun in Toronto, proposed a definition that better describes the nuances required when speaking about Thomism as an historical reality. Weisheipl presents Thomism as "a theological and philosophical movement that begins in the thirteenth century, and embodies a systematic attempt to understand and develop the basic principles and conclusions of St. Thomas Aquinas in order to relate them to the problems and needs of each

15. "Thomism," in *Catholic Encyclopedia,* vol. 14 (New York: Robert Appleton Company, 1912), p. 698.

generation."[16] This definition considers Thomism as a movement whose participants, to the extent that they commit themselves to the characteristically Thomist enterprise of manifesting the rationality of tradition, are able to illuminate and develop the teachings of Aquinas so as to make them useful in addressing the theological concerns of every age.

The present essay proceeds on the assumption that Weisheipl's working definition of Thomism accurately captures what unites those who have associated themselves with the school of Aquinas. It nevertheless remains clear that, throughout its history, some authors approached the "development" of Aquinas's thought with creative fidelity, whereas others adopted a woolly spirit. Development within Thomism can be traced to the *inter-scholas* debates that transpired between Thomists and the adherents of non-Thomist schools, but it has emerged also from *intra-scholam* exchanges within the Thomist school itself. As a result, it is difficult to reach unanimous agreement as to what criteria should be used to identify a particular theologian or philosopher as one who stands within the Thomist circle. Which principles and which conclusions must a scholar accept in order to qualify as a bonafide Thomist? How much may a scholar continue to develop the thought of Aquinas in order to adapt his work to the requirements of a given age, and still remain in continuity with the Thomas Aquinas who died in 1274? Are there limits in the evolution of Thomism that interpreters of Aquinas's works and thought cannot transgress if they wish to remain within the company of mainline Thomists? Theoretical questions such as these have been debated in essays written by con-

16. "Thomism," in the *New Catholic Encyclopedia,* vol. 14 (New York: McGraw-Hill Book Company, 1967), p. 126.

noisseurs of Thomism, although it may be observed that their arguments have produced no conclusive decisions.

There are scholars who question whether it even makes sense to speak about an eight-hundred-year tradition as if it forms a unified school of thought. This radical hermeneutical challenge raises the question whether one may argue that Thomism constitutes a distinctive school of philosophers and theologians. In other words, is it not the case that speaking about a school of Thomism, with its own interpretive tradition, already assumes too much about the way that human understanding mediates between the past and the present? Hans Georg Gadamer[17] has brilliantly raised this question within the larger context of philosophical enquiry, and some Thomists, such as Michel Corbin,[18] have agreed that, since our engulfment in history prohibits achieving a complete reading of any text, claims to absolute objectivity about the meaning of texts therefore are to be excluded. The warning remains salutary, even for those who recognize that this kind of hermeneutical challenge rests on an overly historical view of human understanding. It is true, there are moments of discontinuity in Thomism, but, as the present exercise hopes to make clear, they do not outweigh the substantial unity that informs the Thomist school. This judgment may be made without necessarily endorsing the project of narrowly identifying true Thomists—the which, it is alleged, has sometimes accompanied the efforts of ecclesiastical authorities to encourage Roman Catholic teachers of theology to follow the "mind of Aquinas," this is, to teach *ad mentem Sancti Thomae.*

The variety of interpretations, applications, and concerns that

17. *Wahrheit und Methode* (Tübingen: J. C. B. Mohr, 1965).
18. *Le Chemin de la théologie chez Thomas d'Aquin* (Paris: Beauchesne, 1974).

appear in different ages and among individual Thomists admittedly makes it difficult to formulate one doctrinal synthesis that covers everyone who draws upon the work of Thomas Aquinas. This lack of complete homogeneity does not mean, however, that it is impossible to comment on Thomism, provided that one takes some elementary distinctions into account. For example, Weisheipl distinguishes a "wide" Thomism, which includes anyone who claims to follow the spirit and basic insights of St. Thomas and manifests an evident dependence on his texts, from what he calls "eclectic" Thomism.[19] Wide Thomism is, first of all, easily distinguished from other intellectual traditions and movements such as medieval Augustinianism, Scotism, Protestantism, nominalism, idealism, and materialism. Authors who are shaped by or adopt the foundational tenets of traditions such as these either entirely eschew Thomism or take no interest in what mainline Thomist thinkers have to say; wide Thomism, on the other hand, includes any author who gives the principles and conclusions of Thomas Aquinas a privileged place in the development of his own proper theological or philosophical reflections.

The instances of eclecticism are more difficult to identify, especially since these forms mainly took shape in the modern period, that is, at a time when philosophy began to develop outside of direct ecclesiastical supervision. As a way to cope with the rapid development of humanist learning that the modern period initiated—and one can date this explosion, for practical purposes only, from the mid-sixteenth century—some persons of great intelligence considered it opportune to reconfigure the intellectual de-

19. Weisheipl, "Thomism," p. 127.

sign of Christian theology (and the philosophy that served it) for the purpose of better adapting the Gospel to the thought forms of the new age. A radical expression of this objective can be found in the intellectual work of the major Protestant Reformers, although Christian humanists such as Erasmus of Rotterdam and Jacques Lefèvre d'Etaples offer a more successful example of this correlational strategy. Guy Bedouelle has explained the impact that this Catholic humanist effort, with its emphasis on a return to the sources, *ad fontes,* had on the theological and ecclesiastical culture of the sixteenth century.[20]

During the period of the Catholic Reform, certain Catholic clerics developed a breadth of interest in topics, beyond those of the sacred sciences, which in turn led them to develop a habit of thought that classical Thomists would easily judge as too concrete, and even preoccupied with the particular. A good number of these scholars, such as Francisco Suárez, Luis Molina, and Gabriel Vàzquez, belonged to the then newly established Society of Jesus, but one can also include spiritual authors such as St. Francis De Sales, although admittedly as a man dedicated to the practice of religious devotion he avoided direct entanglements with secular philosophy. Whatever else may be said about this effort to confront modernity, a number of authors who still held Thomas Aquinas as an authority began to work within a larger framework of thought than what up to that point had been considered Thomistic, even if one takes the term in the wide sense. What is distinctive about the efforts of eclectic Thomists is their willingness to import large portions of

20. Guy Bedouelle, "De l'Humanisme aux Reformes," in *L'Aventure de la Réforme,* ed. Pierre Chaunu (Brussels: Editions Complexe, 1991), pp. 95–135.

other philosophical and theological systems so that they are led to relativize the principles and conclusions that constitute the Thomism of Thomas Aquinas. While Suarezianism, Molinism, casuistry, and Salesian spirituality constitute other performative traditions in the history of Western Christianity, they do not warrant full-scale consideration in a history devoted to Thomism.

The eclectic Thomism represented by, among others, certain Jesuits of the modern period blossomed as a result of the Jesuit commitment to higher education and the Society's institutional engagement in the scientific research of the period. This kind of intellectual outreach however entails its own risks, which can open up the way to another form of eclectic Thomism. Alasdair MacIntyre warns of this danger when he cites Thomists who "inadvertently and incautiously accept from other parties to some debate an initial definition of issues and problems that already precludes a genuinely Thomistic outcome. Just this happened," so MacIntyre continues, "when in the late nineteenth century and early twentieth century some Thomists first accepted too easily a Kantian definition of the problems of epistemology and then proposed solutions to those problems that were in fact Kantian rather than Thomistic, generating in the course of so doing that unfortunate hybrid, transcendental Thomism."[21] It thus seems reasonable to conclude that no history of Thomism can include every figure from the Catholic intellectual tradition who turned at some point for inspiration to the writings of Aquinas. To take such an approach would result in composing a history, not of one school of thought, but of almost the entire Christian tradition from the late medieval to the contemporary period.

21. Advice to Thomists, "Thomism and Philosophical Debate," in *The Maritain Notebook* 3.2 (1995), pp. 1–2.

Those who practice Thomism in the strict sense of the term observe a pristine adherence to the central principles of the philosophy and theology that Thomas Aquinas pioneered in the thirteenth century. This means that they eschew large-scale importations from other conceptual systems, while at the same time they aim in their own works to imitate Aquinas's appreciation for the rationality of the tradition. Since certain contemporary thinkers wonder whether it still is possible to identify a body of truths as Thomist, it is useful to identify what it is that recognized scholars generally hold concerning the major principles adopted and the conclusions elaborated by Thomas Aquinas in his writings.

There are factors that make it difficult to establish a judgment about original Thomism with exhaustive precision, and so a few preliminary observations are in order. First, consider Aquinas's works themselves. These compositions include such a broad diversity of literary genres, that to distill common themes from works as dissimilar in kind as biblical exegesis, systematic compendiums, and Aristotelian commentaries makes up a hermeneutical challenge. Furthermore, these same works were written over a period of more than twenty years, during which time Aquinas achieved his own intellectual maturity, and so we can reasonably expect to encounter development of thought even within the *corpus* itself. In fact, Aquinas's earliest adherents noticed that on certain points of theology or philosophy their master spoke better in his *Summa theologiae* than he had earlier in his *Sentences*. One of these, Peter of Bergamo (d. 1482), even produced a concordance whose purpose was to explain apparent contradictions in the works of Aquinas, that is, where "Divus Thomas videtur sibimet contradicere."[22]

---

22. *Concordantiae Textuum discordantium Divi Thomae Aquiniatis* (Florence: Libreria Editrice Fiorentina, 1982).

Another factor to consider is the span of more than seven hundred years that separates the contemporary student of Aquinas from the date of his death. In the course of these centuries, and especially during periods of high interest in the works of Aquinas, many theologians and philosophers have attempted, with more or less success, to interpret his doctrine for their times. This allegiance to Aquinas has produced a long commentatorial tradition that begins especially in the fifteenth century and continues to the twenty-first. While this commentatorial tradition has enjoyed a high degree of success, it also has given rise to disagreements about how to distinguish between what Thomas himself said and what other Thomists have interpreted him to have said. For instance, Prouvost, as we have seen, expounds in a maximum way the discordance between Thomas and his interpreters, so that, on the account of someone like Prouvost, every Thomist stands more by himself than he does in continuity with Aquinas.

These complexities, though real, are not insuperable, and some agreement does indeed exist as to what constitutes the main lines of Thomism. For instance, Leonard A. Kennedy, although he interprets Thomism in a broadly inclusive sense, has produced a catalogue of Thomists who wrote between the years 1270 and 1900.[23] Kennedy, it is true, acknowledges that there are no universally agreed on criteria for answering the question: Who is a Thomist? Instead, he adopts what are described as fairly liberal criteria, such as an indication in the title of a work that the author aims to follow the mind of Aquinas ("ad mentem Divi Thomae"), or that an author produced a book of a certain kind, for example, a commen-

23. *A Catalogue of Thomists, 1270–1900* (Houston: Center for Thomistic Studies, 1987).

tary on one of Aquinas's own works, especially on the *Summa theologiae,* or a statement of alleged Thomism by either the author himself or one of his historians. Using these criteria, Leonard Kennedy lists a total of 2,034 Thomists who worked between the years 1270 and 1900. Before the French Revolution, more than half the Thomists in each century were members of the Dominican Order, but by the time of the nineteenth century Dominicans accounted for only 11 percent of Thomists. Only the Jesuits form another significant group of religious priests who may be numbered among the self-described Thomists. In the nineteenth century, Thomist ranks were swelled by non-religious even before the 1879 publication of *Aeterni Patris.* Kennedy makes no effort to list those who practiced Thomism during the twentieth century, when prior to 1965 the fruits of the revival launched by Pope Leo XIII were especially felt in Europe and the Americas.

The broad criteria that Kennedy employs in his catalogue of Thomists affords the interested party a sweeping view of the Thomist tradition. The large number of catalogued Thomists does not, however, provide the grounds to conclude that every Thomist in one way or another eventually winds up being an eclectic Thomist, at least in the sense in which Weisheipl defines Thomist eclectics. What distinguishes a simple Thomist from an eclectic Thomist? It is safe to conclude that, for the first centuries of Thomism, several key questions in philosophy can serve as bellwethers in order to identify those Thomists who adhered strictly to Aquinas's own principles. The following list of positions, suggested by Weisheipl,[24] includes only those teachings that are philosophical in

---

24. Weisheipl, "Thomism," p. 127.

nature, since it was their confident but judicious use of Aristotelianism in theology that made the earliest Thomists stand out among their contemporaries.

Thomists in the strict sense affirm in the area of natural philosophy that all physical bodies are composed of matter and form, and that only one substantial form actualizes each physical body. They hold further that the individuation of each physical body is achieved by determined matter, and that the separated substances lack any individuating principle. As a corollary, Thomists consider that each angel forms its own unique species. In the area of anthropology, Thomists say that in all created substances, including the sentient and intellective soul, a real distinction exists between the being's activities, which flow from its capacities or faculties, and its essential nature. They further profess that the rational soul remains the unique substantial form of an individual human being. In moral philosophy, Thomists agree that by nature man enjoys the right to dwell in community and to pursue personal happiness within the common good, and that the right conduct of human beings is best described by appeal to the virtues of human life, although laws, both natural and positive, also legitimately direct human action.

The Thomist is best described as a metaphysical realist. There is of course in a certain sense a competition among "the realisms." As some point out, Duns Scotus also may be considered a metaphysical realist.[25] But as Aristotle teaches in the *Metaphysics,* the noblest

25. For example, Serge-Thomas Bonino: "Une affirmation comme 'la meilleure description du thomiste, c'est qu'il est un réaliste métaphysique' (p. 34), convient parfaitement à Duns Scot" in his "Thomistica (VI)," *Revue Thomiste* 100 (2000): 692.

instance within any genus is the cause thereof: and so one may justly assert that the Thomist is preeminently a metaphysical realist insofar as the doctrine of St. Thomas hinges on that which is most formal in being and is its *sine qua non:* the *actus essendi.* Thus understood Thomism remains the noblest and paradigmatic articulation of metaphysical realism. The follower of Aquinas thus judges the conclusions, at least in their classical expression, of both idealism and positivism as untenable. The latter gainsays the existence of universal ideas, at least in the mind of creatures, and the former rejects the epistemological principle that nothing exists in the intellect that was not first in sense knowledge. Thomists defend the reality of creation, and hold the conviction that from the visible things of the universe the human mind can know the existence of God. God enjoys his own subsistent fullness of pure actual being and possesses no limitation of any kind, because nothing of potential is to be found in him. No creature enjoys this status of pure act, and so Thomists espouse what Weisheipl calls the "disturbing distinction" between essence and existence, which entails by way of corollary the conviction that every creature depends on the actuality of borrowed existence. Finally, Thomists think only in terms of analogical predication, such that the metaphysical concept of being is analogically, not univocally, said of God, substances, and accidents. While it is true to say that these positions in philosophy are held by all those who adhere to Thomism in the strict sense of the term, no claim is made that the above list of tenets provides the only theses that Thomists espouse. This brief catalogue of positions, however, does delineate the philosophical views held by a Thomist, to the extent that a given author claims to stand in historical continuity with the teachings of Thomas Aquinas himself.

Since we find a certain consensus among contemporary scholars about which authors adhere strictly to the doctrine of Aquinas and which depart seriously from it for whatever purpose, the above-mentioned themes can serve as partial criteria for sketching the history of Thomism, especially from the late medieval period until the late fifteenth century.

Although in the wake of the sixteenth-century Protestant Reform, Thomism became identified with issues of a predominantly theological character, during the period that followed upon the European revolutions of the late eighteenth and early nineteenth centuries, Thomists again found themselves involved mainly in philosophical issues. The highest authorities of the Roman Catholic Church set a major historical precedent for separation of Thomist from non-Thomist views. This initiative followed the remarkable renewal of Thomism that took place during the long pontificate of Pope Leo XIII (1878–1903).

In the early part of the twentieth century, during the Leonine revival of Thomism, certain ecclesiastical authorities held the view that Aquinas's principles should be expressed in the form of short theses or propositions. Although this objective, undertaken in the aftermath of the Modernist crisis, aimed more toward promoting a sound pedagogy than toward creating a narrow ideology, the Church did give quasi-official recognition to twenty-four theses that were held to embody the essentials of realist philosophy such as one finds in the writings of Thomas Aquinas.[26] The choice to focus on the principles that characterized Thomism in philosophy is explained when one considers the traditional way of referring to

---

26. A. G. Sertillanges, *Les grandes thèses de la philosophie thomiste* (Paris: Bloud & Gay, 1928).

the 1879 encyclical of Pope Leo XIII, *Aeterni Patris:* "On the Restoration in Catholic Schools of Christian Philosophy According to the Mind of the Angelic Doctor Saint Thomas Aquinas." Leonard E. Boyle points out that although the encyclical itself does not carry this title, Pope Leo described it so when on 4 August 1880 he promulgated *Cum hoc sit,* which declared Saint Thomas to be the patron of studies in Catholic schools.[27] The title therefore should not be read with reference to later twentieth-century debates about the nature of Christian philosophy. Instead, the reference to "Christian Philosophy" signals the generally held view that Neo-Thomism was promoted by the Church in response to the widespread use of Cartesian manuals of philosophy that had come to dominate Catholic education, especially seminary training, which use, moreover, was believed to occasion considerable harm to the integrity of the Catholic faith. The initiative of Pope Leo XIII actually promoted a flowering of Catholic intellectual life already underway in the nineteenth century. That century includes more Thomists—756 by Kennedy's count—than any of the previous six centuries.

During the thirty-five years that followed Leo's encyclical, research on the philosophy of Aquinas developed to the point that a consensus existed among certain European thinkers as to what constituted the basics required for Thomism. In other words, Thomism was acknowledged as possessing a recognizable structure. And this agreement made it possible in 1914 for Pope Pius X to direct Catholic professors of philosophy to teach the *fundamenta* and

27. "A Remembrance of Pope Leo XIII: The Encyclical Aeterni Patris," in *One Hundred Years of Thomism,* ed. Victor B. Brezik, C.S.B. (Houston: Center for Thomistic Studies, 1981), pp. 7–22.

principia of Thomism in Catholic universities and colleges. The Pope accomplished this by a *Motu proprio, Doctoris Angelici,* dated 29 June 1914.[28] At the same time, the Sacred Congregation of Studies identified these *fundamenta* as the celebrated Twenty-four Theses of Thomism: "Theses quaedam, in doctrina Sancti Thomae Aquinatis contentae et a philosophiae magistris propositae, adprobantur."[29] It is significant to observe that the Church promoted the doctrine of Aquinas through the agency of what amounts to her Ministry of Education, whose history and present function can be described in terms of an ongoing service to the Truth.[30] At the beginning of the twenty-first century, it is clear that scholars can adequately grasp the significance of this ambitious project only within the context of and as an essential part of the Church's efforts to identify a theological method that would serve the universal call to holiness, which like theology flows from God's simple knowledge of Himself. In other words, the Twenty-four Theses were viewed as an indispensable aid to promoting the Church's mission to fulfill Christ's injunction: "teach them to observe all that I have commanded you" (Mt 28:1).

The hegemony of the Twenty-four Theses over the Church's official pedagogy did not endure for a long time. P. B. Grenet relates that after the death of Pope Saint Pius X, certain difficulties arose that occasioned holding further deliberations as to the binding force of the Twenty-four Theses. So in February 1916, two meetings were held in Rome, which the Belgian philosopher and cardinal

28. *Acta Apostolicae Sedis* VI, 10 [July 1914], 336–41.

29. *Acta Apostolicae Sedis* VI, 11 [August 1914], 383–86.

30. Romanus Cessario, "The Church, Higher Education, and Global Concerns," *Josephinum Journal of Theology* 2 (1995): 25–33.

Désiré Joseph Mercier (1851–1926) attended.[31] Shortly afterwards, the Holy See approved the results of these deliberations by affirming that the Twenty-four Theses ought to be proposed as providing entirely trustworthy norms of direction. Subsequently, the 1917 revision of the *Code of Canon Law* commended to professors of philosophy and theology the methods, doctrine, and principles of the Angelic Doctor, Thomas Aquinas, citing the decree approving the Twenty-four Theses.[32] Later, Benedict XV encouraged the Thomist author Edouard Hugon to compose a commentary on these theses that would explain how they represent the "preferred doctrine of the Church."[33]

Thomism flourished during the period between the two World Wars, and continued to receive papal endorsements after the Second Vatican Council (1962–65), especially by Pope Paul VI, who in 1974, at the close of the ceremonies that marked the seventh centenary of the death of Saint Thomas, addressed a Letter, *Lumen Ecclesiae,* to the Master of the Dominican Order, Vincent de Couesnongle, in which he commended an "authentic fidelity to Thomas."[34] The most recent revision of the *Code of Canon Law* further applauds Saint Thomas Aquinas as a master who can lead students of theology to a deep penetration of the mysteries of salvation.[35] The same theme had appeared in the 1979 Apostolic Consti-

31. *Les 24 Thèses thomistes* (Paris: Librairie P. Tequi, 1962).

32. *Code of Canon Law* (1917), art. 1366, § 2.

33. See R. P. Édouard Hugon, *Principes de Philosophie. Les Vingt-Quatre Thèses Thomistes* (Paris: Pierre Tequi, 1927), p. xv.

34. *Acta Apostolicae Sedis* LXVI [1974], 673–702.

35. *CIC* 252 § 3: "Lectiones habeantur theologiae dogmaticae, verbo Dei scripto una cum sacra Traditione semper innixae, quarum ope alumni mysteria salutis, s. Thoma praesertim magistro, intimius penetrare addiscant. . . ."

tution *Sapientia Christiana,* which governs ecclesiastical universities and faculties, although no attempt of course is made to enforce allegiance to a list of specific theses.[36]

3. CUSTOMARY DIVISIONS IN THE
HISTORY OF THOMISM

It has been customary to recognize three major periods in the history of Thomism: early, or first Thomism, second Thomism, and third, or Neo-Thomism. However, those who have attempted to sketch a history of Thomism are not in full agreement about the proper way to divide these periods chronologically. Réginald Garrigou-Lagrange distinguishes three periods in the history of commentators on the texts of Aquinas.[37] The first, which runs from the end of the thirteenth century through the fifteenth, he calls the period of the *Defensiones,* when early Thomists defended Aquinas's teaching against those who sometimes strongly opposed it. The second period, which covers only the first part of the sixteenth century, he designates that of the *Commentatores* and describes as a time when the attention of Thomists was fixed on Aquinas's systematic treatises, especially the *Summa theologiae,* and on an article-by-article *(articulatim)* explication of these texts. The third period, which Garrigou-Lagrange dates from after the reforms initiated by the Council of Trent to the middle of the eighteenth century, witnesses Thomists engaged in *Disputationes;* that is, after the fashion of dialectical theology they entertained the disputed questions of

36. *Acta Apostolicae Sedis* LXXI [1979], 469–521, esp. Nos. 71 & 80.

37. Réginald Garrigou-Lagrange, "Thomisme," in *Dictionnaire de Théologie Catholique,* t. 15.1, ed. A. Vacant, E. Mangenot, and É. Amann (Paris: Librairie Letouzey et Ané, 1946), cols. 827–31.

their day and seemed to take great delight in responding to a wide range of questions or *dubia*. Writing during the Second World War, Father Garrigou-Lagrange mentions only some of the Thomist authors who wrote after the publication of *Aeterni Patris,* but his overall perspective assumes a continuity in the history of Thomism that often has escaped the notice of other historians. At the same time, even so convinced a Thomist author as Father Garrigou-Lagrange finds nothing of significance on which to remark between the death of the Belgian theologian Charles-René Billuart in 1751 and the revival of Thomism more than a century later under Joachim Pecci, later Leo XIII. By all accounts, Thomism during the eighteenth century entered a holding pattern; even the statistics reveal a decline: there were only 249 Thomists active in *l'âge des lumières* as compared with the 564 who produced Thomist texts—many of them manuals—during the seventeenth century.

The German Thomist Otto Herman Pesch, writing in the early 1960s, adopts Garrigou-Lagrange's divisions but adds a fourth period, that of Neo-Thomism, which he dates from the beginning of the nineteenth century.[38] Other authors, such as the Italian C. Giacon, conceive the history of Thomism mainly in terms of the authors who made use of the texts of Aquinas and so include figures such as Girolamo Savonarola (1452–98), who considered his remarkable apology for orthodox Catholicism, *The Triumph of the Cross,* as nothing other than a compendium of the *Summa contra gentiles.*[39] In Giacon's account of Thomism, authors are categorized

---

38. Otto Herman Pesch, "Thomismus," in *Lexicon für Theologie und Kirche,* Bd. 10, ed. J. Höfer and Karl Rahner (Freiburg: Verlag Herder, 1965), cols. 157–61.

39. C. Giacon, "Tomismo," in *Enciclopedia Filosofica,* 2nd ed., vol. 6 (Roma: G. C. Sansoni, 1968), cols. 505–7.

on the basis of whether they adhered rigidly or with moderation to the thought of Aquinas, and theologians such as the Jesuit Francisco Suárez and Cardinal Bellarmine are described as following Aquinas, "but with a certain liberty of movement." This expression probably amounts to little more than a courteous description of eclectic Thomism.

The venerable English Thomist Thomas Gilby adopts the standard tripartite division of Thomism but introduces some significant points of interpretation that distinguish his account from the way that Garrigou-Lagrange arranges the chronology.[40] Gilby dates the first period of Thomism from the thirteenth to the sixteenth century, and so includes in a single category the early Thomists, who wrote during the first fifty years after Aquinas's death, as well as the Northern Italian commentators of the early sixteenth-century renaissance, such as Cardinal Cajetan and Francis Silvestri (or Ferrariensis). Gilby identifies the second epoch of Thomism as conterminous with the golden age of Spain, the period that he designates as that of the Habsburg Baroque, thereby disclosing more plainly than does Garrigou-Lagrange that by the end of the seventeenth century Thomism flourished principally in centers of ecclesiastical learning. In the third period of Thomism, Gilby includes the nineteenth and twentieth centuries, although he stresses that the modern revival of Thomism began only around the middle of the nineteenth century.

Daniel Ols adopts the divisions first elaborated by the noted historian of Thomas Aquinas, Angelus M. Walz, who had identi-

---

40. Thomas Gilby, "Thomism," in the *Encyclopedia of Philosophy*, vol. 7 (New York: Macmillan Publishing Co., Inc., 1972), pp. 119–21.

fied four periods in the history of Thomism.[41] Walz is the author of a much-consulted study of Aquinas's life and works, *Saint Thomas Aquinas: A Biographical Study.*[42] The Ols-Walz scenario runs as follows: First, primitive Thomism, which extends from the death of Aquinas in 1274 to about 1350, when Thomists defended the thought of Aquinas against the claims advanced by theologians mainly of an Augustinian persuasion, especially by promoting the so-called "correctory" literature *(correctoria).* These authors urged a careful reconsideration of the annotations contained in the *Correctorium fratris Thomae* composed by the English Franciscan William de la Mare, who devised 118 corrections to add to as many questionable passages in Aquinas's works. Ols then identifies a second period of Thomism that runs from the beginning of the fifteenth century (1400) to the middle of the sixteenth (1550), in which he includes the Frenchman John Capreolus (known as the *Princeps Thomistarum),* the North Italian commentators, the forerunners of the Spanish Carmelites at Salamanca (known as the *Salmanticenses*), as well as their fellow countryman and model, the Dominican Francisco de Vitoria (c. 1485–1546). In addition, Ols places within this period the Thomists, mostly Dominicans, who worked at and during the Council of Trent (1545–63), especially the students of Vitoria, Dominic Soto (1494–1560) and Melchior Cano (1509?–69). According to Ols and Walz, the third period should be designated as post-Tridentine Thomism, since it runs from the

41. Daniel Ols, "Tommaso d'Aquino," in *Enciclopedia di Religione,* vol. 5 (Florence: Vallecchi editore, 1973), cols. 1822–25.

42. Trans. Sebastian Bullough (Westminster, Md.: Newman Press, 1951), and the improved French edition with Paul Novarino, *Saint Thomas d'Aquin* (Louvain/Paris: Publications universitaires, 1962).

close of the Council in 1563 until the beginning of the nineteenth century (1800), and so includes those Thomists who died in the seventeenth century, such as Dominic Báñez (1528–1604), John Poinsot (1589–1644), Jean-Baptiste Gonet (d. 1681), and Antoine Goudin (d. 1695). The final period is that of contemporary Thomism, which is said to begin at the end of the nineteenth century,[43] and which Ols claims has pursued objectives that were not fully reconciled one with the other. On the one hand, Thomists undertook historical research into the writings of Aquinas with an eye to determining what constitutes the genuine expression of his thought, and on the other, they sustained a polemical effort, hoping to discover in Thomism the wherewithal to confront modern philosophical positions, especially the deleterious effects of positivism, materialism, and secularism on Catholic beliefs and practices.

We have seen that the several authors who have attempted to construct an outline of Thomism's progression through the centuries offer slightly variant accounts of the divisions that mark the history of Thomism. Each one nevertheless brings out in a particular way the influence that the thought of Thomas Aquinas has exercised on the history of Western Christianity, even outside of the Catholic tradition. Oftentimes the proponents of Aquinas, both those who followed him strictly and those who adopted a more fluid, even eclectic, approach to his works, have found in him a powerful intellectual resource that they could use to uphold the truth of the Catholic religion. When the Second Vatican Council (1962–65) encouraged the Church to adopt an attitude of dialogue with

43. See A. Walz, "Sguardo sul movimento tomista nel secolo XIX final all'enciclica Aet. Patris," *Aquinas* 8 (1965): 315ff.

the modern world, Thomism began to follow, rather suddenly, even abruptly, a new course in its history. In 1974, on the seventh centenary of St. Thomas's death, Pope Paul VI in the Letter already cited summarized the situation of post-conciliar Thomism when he proposed Aquinas as a model to theologians, not only because of the profundity of his doctrine, but also because of his openness to the world and his respect for truth from whatever source.[44] At the beginning of the twenty-first century, Catholic scholars still turn to Aquinas not only for the substance of his thought but also to learn the genius of his standpoint, which to the extent that it introduces them into the "rationality" of the Christian tradition also brings them closer to the wisdom of God.

4. A NEW CONCEPTION OF THIS HISTORY

Given everything that has been said up to this point, one is surprised by the absence of a complete modern treatise on the history of Thomism. The most recent book that attempts to recount the complete history of Thomism was published in 1859, and so does not include the findings that have been the fruit of the revival of medieval scholarship in the twentieth century.[45] What follows, then, mainly relies on articles, monographs, and studies devoted either to specific persons involved in the history of Thomism or to periods when Thomism enjoyed a particular prominence. While the present study purports only to fulfill a provisional objective, it

44. James A. Weisheipl, "Thomas Aquinas," in *The Encyclopedia of Religion,* vol. 14, ed. Mircea Eliade (New York: Macmillan Publishing Company, 1987), pp. 489–90.

45. Karl Werner, *Der heilige Thomas von Aquino,* vol. III: *Geschichte des Thomismus* (Regensburg: G. J. Manz, 1859).

nonetheless provides a sketch of the history of Thomism that will be useful until that day when some scholar with the required time and resources undertakes to research and write the multi-volume history of Thomism that this important school of thought both merits and requires. Perhaps this modest effort to draw together so many diverse strands of a complicated history into a single narrative might even prompt the undertaking of such a full-length study.

The present history of Thomism adopts in a broad sense the perspectives of Father Garrigou-Lagrange, who considered that one can best view Thomism as a continuum of intellectual achievement within the Western theological tradition. No attempt, then, will be made to identify intervals or periods within the larger history of Thomism, or to introduce chronological markers that signal the end of one period and the beginning of another. It is important to stress that this decision implies an evaluative judgment neither about the positive value of Thomism nor about the excellence of Thomists. To put it differently, affirming that Thomism enjoys a continuous history from 1274 to the present moment does not amount to making the claim, as had been made by some Thomists in the neo-scholastic period, that Thomism represents the only approved theology recognized by the Christian Church. Rather, the narration of a continuous history takes into consideration two main facts. First, in the course of their history, Thomists have confronted quite various questions, both in philosophy and in theology; second, the periods of eclipse in the active practice of Thomism can usually be explained by external factors.

First, consider the question of issues. A short review of the issues that engaged Thomism during the past seven centuries reveals that its history flows like a winding river through many different terrains, while its waters pick up sediments from the different geological formations that form its bed. During its nearly eight-hundred-year history, Thomism has influenced nearly every field of human learning, and Thomists have been engaged in widely diverse areas of the intellectual life. For example, in the decades immediately following Aquinas's death, Thomists tackled issues that arose from the introduction of Aristotle into the West: they therefore denied universal hylomorphism and the plurality of substantial forms in the same being, and adopted an "agnostic" attitude toward the eternity of the world, at least from the point of view of scientific demonstration.[46] Later, in the sixteenth century, Spanish Thomists, who constituted a considerable number of the theologians active at the Council of Trent, took on the objections against the Catholic faith that had been advanced by the Protestant divines, answering the difficult claims made against the Church's teaching on justification, the sacraments, and the nature of the Church. Other examples could be cited to show that, throughout the centuries, Thomists occupied themselves with issues that varied as much as mystical theology differs from cosmology, and oftentimes disagreed even among themselves about what it means to think and teach and write on these questions "ad mentem S. Thomae Aquinatis." Nonetheless, what united all these followers of Thomas Aquinas, and continues to unite those who seriously study his works, is the conviction that the teaching of Thomas Aquinas provides a sure guide to the truth of the Christian faith.

---

46. Fernand Van Steenberghen, *Thomas Aquinas and Radical Aristotelianism* (Washington, D.C.: The Catholic University of America Press, 1980).

Second, consider the place of Thomism within the larger setting of Western European history. Since it was not until 1611, when Spanish Dominicans established a university in Manila, that Thomism spread to the New World, we need chiefly to consider the varied fortunes of European intellectual life from 1274 until the present. Although advances in fields related to the sacred sciences, such as the birth of modern science in the seventeenth century, may have affected practicing Thomists less than might have been desired, it remains a safe generalization to say that those times during the past seven centuries when little of note transpired among Thomists were also periods when the practice of theology in general experienced a significant decline.

The historical reasons for widespread intellectual inactivity differ from period to period. For instance, the explanations may stem from physical causes, such as the Black Death that emptied cloisters and university halls not only of students but also of a generation of talented professors. It is generally agreed that the Black Death reduced the population of Europe by as much as one-third, leaving the work of professional education sometimes in the hands of less than fully competent persons. On the other hand, religious dissension, such as followed upon the inception of divisions within Western Christianity, occasioned social upheaval that thwarted the development of Thomism. In some places, Protestantism resulted in the closing of the convents and schools where the Thomist tradition had been studied and passed on. Let two geographical examples suffice: The strong tradition of scholasticism in general and of Thomism in particular that flourished in the British Isles, especially at Oxford, was abolished at the time of the sixteenth-century break with Rome, and only returned there in the early twentieth century when New Blackfriars was opened in Oxford. Likewise, the tradition of Thomist mysticism that flourished in the Rhineland during the late thirteenth and fourteenth centuries and the remarkable enthusiasm for the *Summa theologiae* that succeeded it in the second half of the fifteenth century disappeared in the German principalities that were lost to Rome at the time of the Protestant Reform. This turn of events left Bavarian Benedictine monks as the chief custodians of German Thomism.

On a larger scale, political turmoil often dramatically interrupted the continuation of professional intellectual life, such as happened at the French Revolution, when religious orders—including the Dominicans, who had been the principal carriers of Thomism in the late eighteenth century—were either disbanded or severely restricted in all but a few places in Western Europe. Kennedy lists 166 Dominican Thomists active in the eighteenth century, whereas other religious and non-religious Thomists amounted to half that number.[47] The restoration of the religious orders in France after the French Revolution took time, and their intellectual traditions were not immediately restored to what they had been during the periods of high productivity.[48] Considerations such as these allow one to argue that when Thomism stopped playing an active role in the intellectual life of certain historical periods, the reasons frequently had little to do with the inherent worth of Aquinas's thought or its potential to attract followers. The explanation is to be found in extrinsic factors that inhibited the careful study and appropriation of Aquinas and his texts.

47. Kennedy, *Catalogue*, p. 14.

48. For further information, see *Lacordaire, son pays, ses amis et la liberté des ordres religieux en France*, ed. Guy Bedouelle (Paris: Les Éditions du Cerf, 1991).

There is another reason for recounting the development of Thomism in the form of a continuous narrative. The history of Thomism can as easily be told with reference to geography as it can by following a linear chronology. Thomism of course first moved around Europe, and later spread to the New World as well as to the East. Early Thomism was practiced principally in the university cities of Europe, for it was there that the new mendicant orders sent their students to learn theology. The condemnations of 1277 centered around Paris and Oxford, and the earliest Thomists were gathered around these universities, in addition to those at Cologne, Bologna, and of course Naples. During the first centuries of its existence, Thomism followed the development of the universities in Italy, Spain, Portugal, Germany, Bohemia, Vienna, Cracow, and Louvain. In the period before the Council of Trent and during its sessions the major work of Thomists was carried on in southern France and in northern Italy, whereas in the post-Tridentine period, Thomism flourished principally in the lands of the Habsburgs, especially Spain.

The sixteenth-century *Congregatio de Auxiliis,* which occupied the energies of many Thomists, was in effect a twenty-year conflict among Spanish theologians that generated a two-hundred-year debate between European Jesuits and Dominicans. In the seventeenth century, the conflict over probabilism pitted Thomists against casuists in Spain and against Jansenists in France. Although the impetus behind *Aeterni Patris* came from nineteenth-century Thomists in Germany and Italy, the success of Thomism between 1879 and 1965 extended to most of the European countries and the United States, and even reached as far as the Orient—Far Asian representatives of Thomism include the Japanese scholar Yoshinori

Inagaki. This brief survey of the development of Thomism suggests that there is as much warrant to break down its history into the countries where Thomists worked as into the periods of time in which they lived. In order to avoid introducing secondary questions about epochs and geography, the present history instead chronicles in an uninterrupted fashion the history of Thomism from the time of the death of Aquinas to the last quarter of the twentieth century.

Chapter Two

THE THOMISTS

In one sense, Thomas Aquinas can claim no immediate disciples. The Dominican friars who succeeded to his chair at Paris, Hannibal de Hannibaldis (d. 1272) and Romanus of Rome (d. 1273), both preceded him in death, and neither, in any event, seems to have fathomed the innovations that Aquinas had introduced into theology. His faithful secretary and confessor, Reginald of Piperno, was content, so it appears, with receiving abridged forms of his master's theological *opera,* and there is nothing, moreover, to indicate that he considered himself to be the leader of a newly formed Thomist school. Even those who reasonably may be numbered among the first practicing Thomists, William of Macclesfeld, Giles of Lessines, Bernard of Trilia, and Rambert of Primadizzi, never studied directly under Aquinas. As it happened, Thomism took root and developed amidst controversy rather than from within a circle of supportive friends.

Negative reactions to Aquinas's "innovations," as adherents to the old Augustinian tradition described them, began even during the saint's own lifetime. Aquinas's acceptance of the new Aristotelian learning provoked suspicions that the Dominican master held common ground with the Latin followers of the Spanish Islamic philosopher Averroes, even though Aquinas himself had already exposed the errors of the Averroists that were contrary to the truth of the Catholic religion.[1] So when in 1270, the bishop of Paris, Stephen Tempier, proscribed thirteen problematic theses, whose immediate provenance was the Arts Faculty at Paris, the condemnation cast into a still more unfavorable light the systematic use of Aristotle that Aquinas had introduced into theological debate. Specific issues that fell under Tempier's proscription included the denial both of universal hylomorphism and of the plurality of substantial forms. The Paris ordeal confirms that, in this initial period of Thomism, Aquinas's willingness to dispense with certain older philosophical theories provoked the strongest reactions against his way of doing theology; and, as his opponents included important ecclesiastics, these early protests nearly threatened to subvert the progress of his intellectual achievement. Negative reaction, however, to Aquinas's deployment of Aristotelianism did not stem from disagreement concerning the intrinsic merit of one philosophical viewpoint over another. It happened because it was believed that philosophical theses such as the aforementioned were inextricably bound up with expressing certain truths of the Christian faith. To the extent that Aquinas's antagonists held by and large to the older Augustinian tradition, influenced in some measure by the *Fons vitae* of Avicebron, the condemnation of 1270 can

1. Edward P. Mahoney, "Sense, Intellect, and Imagination in Albert, Thomas and Siger," in *The Cambridge History of Later Medieval Philosophy*, ed. Norman Kretzmann et al. (Cambridge: Cambridge University Press, 1982), pp. 602–22.

safely be said to mark the beginning of the *inter-scholas* debates between Thomists and other traditions in theology. That Bishop Tempier's action was strongly supported by the Franciscans, especially by John Peckham and perhaps even by Saint Bonaventure himself, lends credence to such an historical judgment. Furthermore, this early Franciscan opposition to Aquinas presages later difficulties over theological models between the two mendicant groups.

Aquinas's death did nothing to assuage official fears about his doctrines and his use of Aristotelian philosophy in theology. For shortly afterwards, ecclesiastical authorities in both France and England renewed their condemnations of those theses that seemed to depart from the standard philosophical positions of the old Augustinian school. Thomas Gilby observes that "many of the points at issue were highly technical, and some of them may now seem even trivial; the debate, much of which Thomas himself anticipated in his *Questiones Quodlibetales,* revolves round what to him were contrasts—but to his critics were conflicts—between nature and grace, reason and faith, determinism and freedom, the existence of the universe from eternity and its beginning in time, the soul as biological form and as spirit, and the role of the senses and of divine enlightenment in the acquisition of knowledge."[2] It is worthy of note that the first person to undertake a defense of Aquinas at Paris was his former teacher, Albertus Magnus, who traveled thence in the winter of 1276–77, though to no avail since Bishop Tempier had by the time of Albert's arrival already issued a further condemnation, this time including 219 propositions thought to jeopardize

2. Gilby, "Thomism," p. 119.

authentic instruction in the Christian religion. The large majority of these theses were associated not with Thomas Aquinas himself but with radical Aristotelians like Siger of Brabant, who were heavily influenced by the commentatorial tradition of Averroes.

A few days later on 18 March, Robert Kilwardby, the ex-provincial of the English Dominicans and now archbishop of Canterbury, explaining that he wanted to ensure sound instruction in the schools, proscribed an additional thirty theses, "because" as he explained, "some are manifestly false, others deviate philosophically from the truth, others are close to intolerable errors, and others are patently iniquitous, being repugnant to the Catholic faith."[3] At this juncture, however, Thomist positions received swifter and more developed support than they had at Paris in 1270. Two Dominicans came straightaway to defend Thomist theses and teaching: one was the archbishop of Corinth, Peter of Conflans, who directly protested the Oxford condemnation, and the other was Giles of Lessines, who, in 1278, composed his *De unitate formae,* which successfully argued that substantial form confers only one determinate perfection. This stout Dominican defense of Aquinas mounted some three years after his death marks an important moment in the development of Thomism as a legitimate school of theology within the Christian Church.

Controversy over Aquinas's intellectual legacy, however, did not immediately subside. In the decades following his death, opposition to Aquinas's teaching continued to arise principally among the Franciscans, who considered themselves to be the true guarantors

---

3. D. A. Callus, *The Condemnation of St. Thomas at Oxford,* 2nd ed. (Oxford: Blackfriars, 1955).

of Scripture, Saint Augustine, and Saint Bonaventure. It should be noted that the objections to the new movement, which may be entitled Albertino-Thomism, were softened somewhat by the claim that the real object of contention centered not on Aquinas but on the Averroists. In this context, it is possible to interpret the "emendation" project of William de la Mare as an effort to make Aquinas safe for theological exercises, even though the Franciscan authorities ordained that this scrupulous list of corrections, like the *Summa theologiae* itself, should enjoy a very limited circulation among their friars. Such precautions, however, were insufficient to allay the misgivings that many still held about the Thomist project. The Franciscan archbishop John Peckham, for instance, remained a lifelong opponent of the Thomist position on the unicity of substantial form, even going so far as to excommunicate in 1286 the Dominican Richard Knapwell for holding the view that in man there is only one form, namely, the rational soul and no other substantial form. The intransigency of the position held by Peckham and others was disclosed only twenty-five years later when the fifteenth Ecumenical Council held at Vienne (1311–12) endorsed man's psychophysical unity, affirming that the rational soul serves as the one form of the human body.

Because the intellectual life played such an important role in shaping the ethos of the early Dominicans, Benedict Ashley characterizes the primitive friars as "professors."[4] During the last quarter of the thirteenth century, these learned men formed the first cadre of active Thomists. Kennedy catalogues 40 Thomists in the thirteenth century, of whom 37 were members of the Dominican

4. Benedict Ashley, O.P., *The Dominicans* (Collegeville, Minn.: The Liturgical Press, 1990).

Order. Indeed by the time that the Dominican General Chapter met at Paris in 1286, the Order was already poised to defend and promote Thomist teachings, and successive such chapters sustained this unreserved approbation of Aquinas's methods and texts. The Dominican Order's espousal of Thomism also received the support of the Roman Curia, which for ecumenical reasons was, at that time, inclined favorably toward Greek learning. Since the chief legislative body of the Dominican Order obliged every one of its members "insofar as he was able and capable, to devote himself effectively to the study, promotion and defense of the doctrine of the venerable master, friar Thomas de Aquino, of celebrated memory,"[5] it seems reasonable to date the *intra-scholam* development of Thomism from the last decades of the thirteenth century. Later, the canonization of Saint Thomas in 1323 added new impetus to make Thomism the official teaching to be observed by conventual lectors and masters of theology in the educational institutions sponsored by the Dominican Order. It is true that in the decades following Aquinas's death, Carmelite masters, such as Gerard of Bologna and John Baconthorpe, and the Cistercian Humbert of Preuilly took up certain Thomist themes—though with less consistency than did the Dominicans—still, the earliest exchanges among Thomists transpired within the Order to which Aquinas himself belonged.

The Dominicans had arrived in England during the first quarter of the thirteenth century, and immediately founded convents at Canterbury, London, and Oxford. The first Dominican theologian at Oxford was Robert Bacon (d. 1248), who apparently followed

5. A. Walz, "Ordinationes capitulorum generalium de Sancto Thoma eiusque cultu et doctrina," *Analecta ordinis Praedicatorum* 16 (1923–24): 169–70.

the standard Augustinianism of his day. By the end of the thirteenth century, however, Thomism had taken firm root in the British Isles. In a study that merits more attention than it has received, F. J. Roensch provides an exhaustive account of the earliest disciples of Aquinas in England and France.[6] His research reveals that the debates between Franciscans and Dominicans set the agenda in England for Thomist theologians, even though the variety of apostolic works in which these early English Thomists were engaged requires that one understand "school" in a broad sense, and not according to the modern usage, as when one speaks of the British analytical school or l'École des chartes. For example, it is illustrative to note that whereas the Dominican provincial superior and later archbishop of Dublin (although he died before reaching his see) William of Hothum (d. 1298) composed the standard scientific writings of a medieval regent master, namely, a commentary on the *Sentences,* sermons, philosophical commentaries, and quodlibetal questions, he was obliged for the better part of his career to serve the English Crown as an agent for political affairs.

Hothum is best known for his defense of Richard Knapwell (d. 1288)—that hapless champion of the unicity of substantial form who ran afoul of the tradition-bound Archbishop of Canterbury. In his work entitled *Correctorium corruptorii fratris Thomae,* the correction of the corrupters of brother Thomas, Knapwell further demonstrated his Thomist convictions by giving a quick riposte to the Franciscan-inspired *Correctorium.* Knapwell's unhappy career reveals the pugnacity that sometimes characterized the earliest *inter-scholas* exchanges. In his case, a promising academic career was

6. *Early Thomistic Schools* (Dubuque, Iowa: The Priory Press, 1964).

cut short by his enforced departure from Oxford as well as by his inability to win a reversal of his condemnation from Pope Nicholas IV, who, it should be noted, earlier had made profession in the Franciscan Order. Knapwell's censure did prompt the Dominican Order to adopt a pro-active position with respect to promoting the doctrine of Aquinas, and so he enjoyed the consolation of knowing that his troubles at least bore good fruit.

Other early English Thomists were less caught up in the perils of political machinations. The considerable literary output of Robert Orford, about whom little is otherwise known, reveals that Thomism early on attracted men of intelligence. These were prepared to mount a stout defense against some of Aquinas's classical opponents, especially the Parisian masters Giles of Rome and Henry of Ghent. The better-known Thomas Sutton (d. 1315?) achieved an even higher profile as a result of his expository treatises on philosophical subjects. He may enjoy the privilege of being the first Thomist to address critically the work of John Duns Scotus, the Franciscan doctor whose name would become for the Franciscan school what that of Thomas Aquinas is for the Dominican.[7] Sutton even completed two commentaries on Aristotle, on the *Perihermeneias* and the *De generatione,* that Aquinas had left unfinished. On the other hand, William of Macclesfeld (d. 1303), a contemporary of Sutton, represents an English Dominican Thomist who, in his *Contra Corruptorem Sancti Thomae,* successfully defended the Thomist school theses against William de la Mare and other Franciscans, though without suffering the dire consequences

---

7. George Marcil, "The Franciscan School through the Centuries," in *The History of Franciscan Theology,* ed K. B. Osborne (St. Bonaventure, N.Y.: The Franciscan Institute, 1994), pp. 311–30.

that befell his senior Richard Knapwell. This springtime of English Thomism, however, did not proceed unabated. After 1320, the teaching of the Franciscan William of Ockham began to gain influence within intellectual circles, especially in England, though as late as the beginning of the 1400s we find the Dominican Thomas of Claxton (d. 1415?), who composed his *Quaestiones de distinctione inter esse et essentiam reali atque de analogia entis* at the start of the century, still holding his ground on classical Thomist theses such as the real distinction of essence and existence *(esse)* and the analogy of being.

On both sides of the English Channel, the new mendicant friars fell in easily among the university class. In Paris, the Dominican friars lived under the patronage of the Apostle James—thus the title Jacobin for a Dominican friar—and from the convent of Saint-Jacques they played an active role in the political and intellectual life of the University of Paris. Bernard of Trilia (d. 1292), a junior contemporary of Aquinas, occupies the first place, chronologically, among French Thomists. His literary output reveals a man of general intelligence—*Sentence* commentary, disputed and quodlibetal questions, sermons, and expositions of Scripture—while his positions on the role of sense knowledge in human knowing and on the body-soul composite clearly earn him a place among Aquinas's worthy followers. Another continental Dominican, the Belgian Giles of Lessines (d. 1304?), may have studied under both Albertus Magnus and Aquinas; in any event he surely was personally acquainted with them. Because of Giles's strong defense of the unicity of substantial form, he is remembered as an early Thomist activist, and, moreover, he was probably instrumental in soliciting the aid of Albertus Magnus when the Parisian authorities began to question the legitimacy of Aquinas's use of Aristotelianism. Not every Thomist, however, was a member of Aquinas's own order. There were also secular masters, such as Peter of Auvergne (d. 1304), who, like Giles of Lessines, undoubtedly knew Aquinas during his second Parisian regency. Peter's collection of philosophical and theological writings demonstrates both his adherence to Aristotelian thought and his acceptance of Aquinas as a master, although scholars dispute the extent to which (for example, in his *In libros Metaphysicorum*)[8] he adheres closely to each of Aquinas's tenets.

John Quidort (d. 1306) was a Dominican of Parisian provenance whose clerical career in that university city did not prevent him from becoming involved in a complete range of apostolic activities. By the beginning of the fourteenth century, Quidort had already strongly defended nascent Thomism in his *Correctorium "Circa,"* a theological summary of the first sections of Aquinas's *Summa theologiae* composed to respond to the latter's Franciscan critics. John continued to write on a broad variety of subjects, and therefore contributed to the refinement of Thomist thought on some of the traditional theses, such as the unicity of form and the composition of *esse* with essence in created things, as well as the development of Thomist views on issues such as the separation of Church and state that began to take on new relevance in the fourteenth century. On certain theological topics, however, Quidort was less faithful to his master's teaching, which may account for why he was twice censured for his views on the mode of existence that Christ's body enjoys in the Eucharist. Despite these small departures from the thought of St. Thomas, Gilby considers John

8. "*Quaestiones in Metaphysicam Petri de Alvernia,*" ed. Arthur Monahan in *Nine Mediaeval Thinkers*, ed. J. R. O'Donnell (Toronto: PIMS, 1955), pp. 145–81.

Quidort of Paris equal in stature to Thomas Sutton as an outstanding promoter of nascent Thomism.

Thomism grew because it was supported by a group of brilliant professors who understood the breakthrough that Aquinas had achieved in Christian theology. Because he represents the theological status quo of thirteenth-century Paris, Henry of Ghent—who belonged to no religious order—best illustrates the general approach to theology that these first Thomists rejected. Born in Ghent, probably in the first quarter of the thirteenth century, Henry studied at Tournai at the cathedral school there, where he was canon by 1267. Thereafter, he apparently studied arts at Paris and continued his studies in the faculty of theology. By 1276, Henry was a regent master in the Paris faculty of theology, where he continued to teach until his death in 1293. He was appointed archdeacon of Bruges in 1277 and archdeacon of Tournai in 1279. During this time, too, he was involved in the commission instituted by Bishop Tempier to examine the orthodoxy of teaching at the University of Paris. The commission's work formed the basis for the condemnation of 1277. Henry was strongly opposed to the mendicant privilege to hear confessions and voiced concerns frequently in the 1280s. One may safely say that at the time of his death he was the most prominent theologian in Europe, having attained a fame that, at least in theology, rivaled that of Thomas Aquinas.

Early continental Thomists sharpened their dialectical skills by taking issue with the theological positions developed by Henry of Ghent. In particular, the Dominican Bernard of Auvergne engaged in a polemical rebuttal not only against Henry of Ghent but also against his student Godfrey of Fontaines, who, beginning in 1285, served as master in the theology faculty for some fifteen years.

Bernard became a source of Thomism for renaissance humanists such as Pico della Mirandola, and thereby secured a place in the history of Thomism, one that symbolizes the successful introduction into Western theology of the distinctions between essence and existence, matter and form, substance and accident. Henry of Ghent also dealt with these philosophical themes in theology, but without, so it seems, fully disengaging himself from the older Augustinian conceptions that demarcate the frontiers that Aquinas crossed. Étienne Gilson wrote at the middle of the twentieth century that "the history of the kind of Augustinianism represented by Henry of Ghent has not yet been studied."[9] Even so in the view of some scholars, the theological project of John Duns Scotus and his followers instantiates a highly innovative expression of this history.[10]

Henry of Ghent's critic, Bernard of Auvergne, epitomized the controversialist, whereas his fellow Dominican Harvey Nedellec (d. 1323) exemplified the practicing theologian, albeit one engaged in lively controversy with his contemporaries. Nedellec (in Latin, Hervaeus Natalis) produced over forty works in theology and philosophy. However, Weisheipl opines that since Harvey had studied Aristotle before entering the Dominican Order, he never fully grasped the Thomistic distinction between essence and existence in creatures. As Harvey's scholastic title, *Doctor rarus,* suggests, he

9. *History of Christian Philosophy in the Middle Ages* (New York: Random House, 1955), pp. 452–53. Since Gilson made this remark, the situation has somewhat changed; for instance, see the work of Roland J. Teske, S.J., *Henry of Ghent: Disputed Questions on Free Will* (Milwaukee: Marquette University Press, 1993).

10. Armand A. Maurer, *Medieval Philosophy* (New York: Random House, 1962).

possessed an intellectual character of such uniqueness that it may have isolated him from sharing in the enthusiasms of other early Thomists. Still, sometime in the first decade of the fourteenth century, Harvey did compose his *Defensio doctrinae fr. Thomae,* which inaugurates a genre of Thomistic literature that, in the next century, would achieve new expression in the erudite and innovative compositions of John Capreolus.

The Dominican Order enjoyed rapid growth not only in England and France but also in Italy and Germany. In the last quarter of the thirteenth century, the Bolognese Rambert of Primadizzi (d. 1308) composed his *Apologeticum contra corruptorium Sancti Thomae* as his own peculiar contribution to the *Correctorium* literature. Other Italians, notably Bartholomew of Lucca, who was both student under and companion of Aquinas, and John of Naples, master in theology at Paris in 1315, were especially active in promoting both the virtues and the theses of their fellow countryman, although John failed to grasp the importance that individuation by quantified matter held in Aquinas's metaphysics. In general, the Italians took a dim view of the condemnations of 1277, and they proceeded without hesitation to rely on the theology of Aquinas. However, their signal contributions to the development of emerging Thomist thought occurred in the areas of practical theology: Albert of Brescia composed a pastoral handbook, *De officio sacerdotis;* Bartholomew of San Concordio drew up a summary of ethics, *Compendium philosophiae moralis;* and Rainier of Pisa produced an alphabetized dictionary of theology entitled *Pantheologia.* Pastoral works such as these demonstrate that the value of Thomism was not limited to the university classroom, but was also recognized as a source of eminently practical wisdom for everyday Christian living. The witness of Antoninus Pierozzi (1379–1459), archbishop of Florence from 1446, crowns this stream of wise practical Thomism. His *Summary of Moral Theology,* which is the first treatise of this type, combines three volumes that interpret the speculative wisdom of Aquinas's distinctive presentation of Christian moral teaching with another volume on the moral responsibilities of persons in the different states of life.

In Germany, the Thomist tradition followed its own peculiarly creative course. The disciples and spiritual heirs of Albert the Great continued to cultivate the mystical and Neoplatonic elements of his writings even after they began to read Aquinas. Their *Sentence* commentaries and disputed questions reflect the emphasis on the hierarchical structures of earth and heaven that Albert adapted from the writings of Pseudo-Dionysius. Gilson speaks about the neoplatonizing direction of the German Dominican school, whereas the historian Martin Grabmann[11] describes the following German scholars as the earliest representatives of Thomism *tout court:* John of Sterngassen, author of a *Sentence* commentary and quodlibetal questions; Gerard of Sterngassen, who wrote a pastoral *vademecum*; and Nicholas of Strassburg, a preacher who also composed a *Summa philosophica,* and who, moreover, borrowed extensively from the Frenchman John Quidort, or so it is alleged. Also in the fourteenth century, John of Lichtenberg helped champion the *Summa theologiae* as a textbook for theology, and the little-known Dominican Henry of Lübeck adopted an irenic approach to theological differences when he openly argued for interpreting Augustine on the problem of the divine co-operation with creatures "secundum doctorem Thomam"—according to master Thomas.

Later German Thomists, who even more generously availed

---

11. See his *Mittelalterliches Geisteleben,* 3 vols. (Munich: M. Hueber, 1925–56).

themselves of the Neoplatonic elements that Albertus Magnus had mined from not only Pseudo-Dionysius the Areopagite but also the Islamic philosopher Avicenna, include Ulrich of Strasbourg, Dietrich of Freiberg, and Berthold of Moosburg. Timothy Noone rather insists that these three authors clearly "belong to the quite distinct school of Albertism, though, equally clearly, they exercised considerable independence of mind even in regard to Albert's teaching."[12] Similarly, Serge-Thomas Bonino wonders whether "le trés antithomiste Dietrich de Freiberg" even merits a place among Thomists.[13] There is reason then to question the tendency to classify later Dominican thought as Thomistic whether it genuinely is or not. The caution applies particularly to Meister John Eckhart (d. 1328). This German mystic so adapted his Thomist learning, which he nonetheless cherished, by employing a radically negative or apophatic theological method, that some twenty-eight propositions excerpted from his works merited a serious, though posthumous, papal condemnation.[14] To the extent that Eckhart wholeheartedly appropriated a conceptual scheme of metaphysics that has its roots in the writings of Proclus, whom Eckhart in fact cites, in addition to those of Pseudo-Dionysius, the *Liber de causis,* and some relevant texts from Avicenna, this Dominican, *"homo doctus et sanctus"* though he was, veered away from the general directions that Thomism took in the fourteenth century.

Parisian-style Thomism continued to flourish in the fourteenth

12. See his review of the French edition, *The Thomist* 65 (2001): 139–40.

13. *Revue Thomiste* 100 (2000): 692. But for another view, see William A. Wallace, *The Scientific Methodology of Theodoric of Freiberg: A Case Study of the Relationship between Science and Philosophy,* Studia Friburgensia, N.S. 26 (Fribourg: The University Press, 1959).

14. Robert E. Lerner, "New Evidence for the Condemnation of Meister Eckhart," *Speculum* 72 (1997): 347–66.

century, especially during the period of the Avignon papacy (1309–77), when the Roman Pontiffs were obliged to rely on the services of many Dominicans. Because the papal court had moved to French soil, the principal protagonists of course were French. Armand de Belvézer (1340) worked in the curia of John XXII, even though he like all Thomists rejected this Pope's personal theological view on the beatific vision, which supposed that the souls of the just must await the moment of the Final Judgment in order to enjoy beatitude. The Dominican Peter of La Palu (Palude, d. 1342), another friar active in the service of the Avignon papacy, found time nonetheless to address the nominalizing tendencies that cropped up as a result of Ockham's influence. In addition, Palude was able to pronounce on certain new issues that emerged in the first half of the fourteenth century, especially the relationship between papal and regal power, the privileges of mendicants, and Franciscan poverty. William Peter Godinus (d. 1336) stands out as one who exemplifies the best tradition of medieval Thomism, as demonstrated by his widely used *Lectura Thomasina,* a commentary on the *Sentences.* (This unpublished work was doubtless one of the standard presentations of Thomistic thought until the advent of Capreolus; its publication would do much to illuminate the intellectual history of the fourteenth century.) During the controversies that developed in the wake of claims made by the Franciscan Spiritualists that the imitation of Christ's poverty admits only of a radically absolute interpretation, William successfully introduced some helpful distinctions that saved the evangelical counsel from being practiced by only a few. In addition, William served important ecclesiastico-political missions for Pope John XXII and was influential in arranging for the canonization of Thomas Aquinas by the same Pontiff on 18 July 1323.

The canonization of Thomas Aquinas not only announced his holiness, but also vindicated the saint's intellectual work. The convalidation of Aquinas's theology was solemnly confirmed in 1325 during a convocation of Parisian masters presided at by the bishop of Paris, Stephen Bourret, who revoked his predecessor's condemnation insofar as it "touched or seemed to touch the teaching of blessed Thomas."[15] The general decline of learning and religious life in the second half of the fourteenth century affected adversely the *intra-scholam* development of Thomism, although the *inter-scholas* exchanges continued to advance along increasingly settled party lines. In other words, Thomism remained matched against Scotism and nominalism, even if some prominent Dominicans, such as the French bishop Durandus of Saint-Pourçain and the Cambridge master Robert Holkot, clearly broke ranks.

The facts of Durandus's early life are not well known, but his later career offers a glimpse of the intellectual climate in which fourteenth-century Thomism had to survive. Although a Dominican friar by profession, Durandus became a bishop in 1317. His status however did not preserve him from the scrutiny of the Dominican Order, whose authorities considered his *Commentary on the Sentences* to contain more than a few—235 altogether—positions that were opposed to Aquinas's teaching. He thus became the object of several censures by the Order, so that he was obliged to produce a corrected version of his *Commentary,* which alone survives in the printed editions. Despite his own nominalistic leanings, Durandus was part of the commission that examined certain positions

15. For how this action affected education among the Dominicans, see M. Michèle Mulchahey, *"First the Bow is Bent in Study": Dominican Education before 1350* (Toronto: Pontifical Institute of Mediaeval Studies, 1998), p. 160.

of William of Ockham and found fifty-one of them wanting. Durandus's own position in epistemology falls decidedly outside of the Thomist school, but it is generally agreed that it is difficult to characterize the thought of this original, and sometimes obstinate, thinker. We do know, however, that Thomists did not allow Durandus's views to go unchallenged, as refutations such as the *Evidentiae Durandelli contra Durandum,* by a friar known to us only as "Durandellus," demonstrate. Gilson concludes that Durandus himself "was not born to be a Thomist because his mind inhabited another intellectual country, which it is not easy to describe and still less to classify."[16] In any event, Durandus, or more specifically his case, illustrates the difficulty that Thomists faced in sustaining Aquinas's enterprise of integrating a wide-ranging philosophy with theology.[17]

The Great Western Schism (1378–1417) and the disastrous consequences of the Black Death, an outbreak of bubonic plague that killed about 25 million people after its first occurrence in 1347, seriously affected the social fabric of the European continent, leaving no institution unaffected by either division or diminishment or both. It is significant, however, to note that during roughly the same period when the practice of the intellectual life began to decline in those countries where in the previous century it had flourished, Thomism was taking fresh root outside of Western Europe in places such as Byzantium. The evidence for the flourishing of Byzantine Thomism is mostly literary: Maximus Planudes translated Aquinas's *Super symbolum apostolorum* into Greek, Gregory Akindynos translated part of the *Summa contra gentiles* into Greek,

16. Gilson, *History,* p. 476.
17. For more information, see Mulchahey, *First,* pp. 153–60.

Prochoros Kydones wrote a treatise *De esse et operatione* and translated the *De eternitate mundi* into Greek, as Demetrios Kydones did for the *Summa contra gentiles,* certain *opuscula,* and the *Summa theologiae.* In general, it is safe to assert that Thomism spread beyond its original environment along with the rapid expansion of the mendicant friars, especially the Dominicans. By the end of the fourteenth century, Thomist authors can be found working in Armenia, Bohemia, Poland, Scandinavia, and Spain; in short, the Thomist school became active in places beyond the university centers of Cologne, Oxford, Paris, and Bologna.

The preservation of Aquinas's works and the continuance of his thought owes a great deal in the late Middle Ages to the religious reform of the Dominican Order carried out under Blessed Raymond of Capua (1330–99). The latter half of the fourteenth century, it is true, witnessed difficult circumstances in every sphere of life, but the multiplication of manuscripts during this same period suggests continued and even increasing interest in Aquinas's compositions, even though the main lines of his teaching did not go uncontested. In fact, there arose during this period one of the most notorious controversies, which for succeeding centuries would distinguish Thomist theologians from those belonging to other schools. It concerned the doctrine of the Immaculate Conception of the Blessed Virgin Mary, on which Aquinas followed the same hesitant opinion that holy men such as Bernard of Clairvaux and Saint Bonaventure had adopted. This hesitancy arose from the worry that to suppose the remission of original sin in anyone before the actual moment when Christ won it by his life, death, and resurrection would inextricably lead to a relativization of the Paschal mystery. The Franciscans who followed Scotus, however, spoke about Mary's sanctification as "preventative" so that she came into personal existence not in sin but in grace. The solemn definition of Pius IX in 1854 made a direct reference to Christ's "foreseen merits," and so combined the insights of both traditions. In the intervening centuries, however, a flood of literature from Dominicans who, after the official approbation of Aquinas as the Doctor of the Order, felt obliged to defend his position was met by a counter flood of literature from the Franciscans.[18]

While schoolmen such as William of Ockham, Peter Aureolus, and John Duns Scotus dominated the late medieval period, the Dominican John Capreolus emerged as the champion of a small, anti-revisionist movement that, in effect, became a nucleus of the Thomism that during the Italian renaissance flourished in its own circles and even influenced certain secular humanists. Kevin White reports that although Capreolus is associated with the French city of Rodez, the relevant documents refer to him more frequently as *Tholosanus* ("of Toulouse") than as *Ruthenensis* ("of Rodez").[19] The name "Capreolus"—meaning "little goat" or "the kid"—seems to be a local Latinizing coinage, one also found in the Rouergue in the forms "Cabrole" and "Cabrolier," though it is unknown whether "John" is his baptismal name or a religious name adopted on his en-

18. Ashley, *Dominicans,* p. 68.

19. See "Translators' Introduction" in John Capreolus, *On the Virtues,* trans. Kevin White and Romanus Cessario, O.P. (Washington, D.C.: The Catholic University of America, 2001), p. xxviii. This may be explained by the fact that the Dominican house in Rodez, where Capreolus joined the Order, belonged to the Dominican province of Toulouse, and by the fact that Capreolus was for a time regent of studies at the house in Toulouse. It is in any case certain that Capreolus was born either in the village of Rodez or in the surrounding region, known as "the Rouergue."

try into the Dominican Order. What is known, however, is that Capreolus attained his religious maturity in the Midi of France, which since 1386 had become in a deeply symbolic sense the spiritual center of Thomism. It was in that year that Pope Urban V decreed that the relics of Thomas Aquinas be transferred from Italy to a shrine erected in the Church of the Jacobins in Toulouse.

On May 15, 1407, the Dominican general chapter at Poitiers ordered Capreolus to proceed to the University of Paris to comment on Peter Lombard's *Book of Sentences.* In 1409 he completed the first book of his life's work, *The Books of Arguments in Defense of the Theology of Saint Thomas Aquinas,* a work which, from one point of view, may be regarded as a highly innovative contribution to the Parisian tradition of commentaries on the *Book of Sentences.* In 1411 and 1412 he took examinations for the Licentiate in Theology, passing with a standing of twelfth place, but first place among all mendicants, in his class of twenty-five. After these examinations Capreolus may have stayed on in Paris, or he may have gone back to Rodez, to which he certainly had returned by 1426. At some point during the period 1412–26 he served as regent of studies in Toulouse. Back in Rodez in 1426, Capreolus concentrated his efforts until 1432 on finishing his great work. After completing all of his *Defense,* Capreolus lived for another twelve years, remaining at Rodez, and dying in 1444.[20]

Capreolus's massive accomplishment forms a significant juncture in the history of Western theological literature. His analysis on the one hand looks to the past, especially to the disputes that Thomists undertook with Scotists and Ockhamists, and on the

20. White and Cessario, translators, *On the Virtues,* contains the largest (nine questions) available English translation of the *Defensiones.*

other, his systematization of Thomist themes prepares the way for the important contributions that Thomist theologians made during the period of the Catholic Reform in the sixteenth century and again after the Leonine renewal that began in the late nineteenth century. In the context of fifteenth-century theology, Capreolus conducted an exercise in the traditional genre of question-commentaries on Lombard's *Book of Sentences,* a work which was composed during the 1150s and had been the official "textbook" of theology at Paris since 1225. Many of his Thomist predecessors had used this same kind of writing—*scriptum super libros Sententiarum*—to advance specifically Thomist theses, just as their opponents had done to disseminate Scotist and nominalist positions. The typical question-commentary on the *Sentences* proceeds by raising, and in each case considering both sides of, questions in some way related to the various units or "distinctions" in each of the four books of Lombard's work: the first book concerns God, the second creation, the third Christ and the virtues, and the fourth "the last things." But while the *Sentences* thus provided a scaffolding that indicates an order of topics and suggests the content of questions, it more often than not served as a pretext and occasion for the introduction of questions of current interest in theological circles but only remotely connected to Lombard's own concerns. Both the brilliance of the *Defensiones* and the fact that it embodies the first comprehensive presentation of Thomist theology merited Capreolus, as we have seen, the title *Princeps Thomistarum,* the Prince of Thomists.

Capreolus's use of Lombard's *Sentences* as a starting-point to provide his own theological commentary reflects the enduring value of this twelfth-century theology textbook, which was used, moreover, in some schools of theology even up to the end of the eighteenth century. During the second half of the fifteenth century, however, the *Summa theologiae* gained ascendency as the standard textbook for professors of theology, especially in those German universities where Dominicans taught. Among the earliest Summists, J. O. Riedl[21] names Gerard of Elten (d. 1484) for his commentary on the *prima pars* of the *Summa theologiae,* while Anton Michelitsch[22] points to Kaspar Grunwald (fl. 1490), who may in fact have been the first to produce a complete commentary on the *Summa.* As a rule, these commentaries were developed from the lessons in theology that senior Dominican lectors had first delivered in their own convents to the student-friars. This commentatorial tradition continued without interruption until the Reformation. For instance, Conrad Köllin (d. 1536), who attained prominence and influence even outside of his native Germany, in part because he was one of the first Catholic theologians to take issue with Martin Luther's teaching on marriage, had published in 1512 a celebrated commentary on the *prima-secundae* of Aquinas's *Summa.*

Germany was not the only country that witnessed the flourishing of a vigorous intellectual life. By the fifteenth century, the Low Countries, the duchy of Burgundy, and the Franche Comté—all domains of Charles the Bold (1433–77), last duke of Burgundy— had become regions renowned for their high cultural achievements, including the areas of ecclesiastical learning. The Belgian

21. *A Catalogue of Renaissance Philosophers* (Milwaukee: Marquette University Press, 1940).

22. *Kommentatoren zur Summa Theologiae des hl. Thomas von Aquin* (Graz: Styria, 1924).

theologian Denis the Carthusian (d. 1471) offers a good example of the latter to the extent that this "ecstatic doctor" combined a comprehensive treatment of Aquinas's theology with a retrieval of biblical science and patristic learning, modeling the kind of return-to-the-sources theology that would revitalize Thomism at other moments in its history. On the other hand, Dominic of Flanders (d. 1479), who spent a large part of his life teaching in Northern Italy, concentrated on philosophy, writing an important commentary on Aristotle's *Metaphysics,* which he dedicated to Lorenzo de Medici, as well as other philosophical treatises. Elsewhere, Thomists who continued in the commentatorial tradition produced special treatises on theological subjects that had begun to excite controversy in theological circles. For example, the Hungarian Dominican Nicholas de Mirabilibus (fl. c. 1500) composed his essay *De predestinatione* in order to elucidate Thomist teaching on a topic that would occupy the energies of Thomists well into the eighteenth century. During this transition period between the Middle Ages and the Renaissance, Thomism demonstrated that it possessed the interior vitality required to engage new questions in theology, and at the same time to continue to lead its adherents toward a deeper penetration of the "rationality of tradition," which distinguished Aquinas in his own encounter with the philosophy and theology that preceded him.

The consolidation of Habsburg political power, with its strong commitment to Catholic learning and piety, exerted a significant impact on the development of Thomism. The domination began after Maximilian I became Holy Roman Emperor in 1493, and reached a high point in the first half of the sixteenth century when, as a result of shrewd diplomacy and marriage policy, his grandson

Charles was able to exercise an unparalleled political hegemony over Spain and its overseas empire, parts of Italy, the Netherlands, and the Habsburg German and Austrian possessions. In the first decade of the sixteenth century, the Belgian Peter Crockaert, whose personal evolution from secular Ockhamist to Dominican Thomist reveals the fluidity of the period, introduced the *Summa* as a textbook for theologians at Paris, and subsequently his student, Francisco de Vitoria, did the same twenty years later at the Spanish university of Salamanca. Of course, once Aquinas's works became available in printed editions, the use of the *Summa* and the distribution of commentaries on it were greatly facilitated.

Recent scholarship has contributed much to illuminating the role that Thomist scholasticism played in the development of sixteenth-century Renaissance thought. Paul Oskar Kristeller states that "on the whole, the Thomism of the Dominican school presented itself during the Italian Renaissance as a current of thought whose solidity and strength were felt in the theological and philosophical debates of the time and which likewise exerted a certain influence outside the framework of the Order."[23] The view that the medieval tradition contributed something positive to the humanist renaissance of the sixteenth century challenges the prevailing opinion in vogue since the Enlightenment, which solemnly declared that the *studia humanitatis* provided a clear-cut intellectual alternative to what the immediately preceding centuries had cultivated. In his study of early classical science, William A. Wallace has demonstrated that something similar took place in the field of

23. "Thomism and Italian Thought," in *Medieval Aspects of Renaissance Learning: Three Essays by Paul Oskar Kristeller,* ed. and trans. Edward P. Mahoney (New York: Columbia University Press, 1992), p. 51.

natural science, especially in light of the pronounced scholastic influences on Galileo Galilei that scholars have recently documented.[24]

A school of Northern Italian Thomists, who worked mainly at Padua and Bologna, distinguished itself for both erudite studies of and commentaries on Aquinas's works. One of its leaders, Peter of Bergamo, in addition to his concordance, constructed the *Tabula aurea,* which remained the only complete index to the works of Saint Thomas until the dawn of the computer age when another Northern Italian, Roberto J. Busa, S.J., produced his *Index Thomisticus.* And there were still other Thomists whose works published in the last quarter of the fifteenth century reveal a vibrant intellectual life in the decades immediately preceding the Protestant reform. To cite just one example, Peter Nigri (d. 1483), sometime rector of the University of Budapest, wrote his strongly polemical treatise, *Clypeus Thomistarum,* which was published in Venice in 1481. The Italian peninsula also witnessed an interest in Aquinas on the part of those outside ecclesiastical circles. Many of the Aristotelians and other lay philosophers who dominated university teaching, especially Pietro Pomponazzi, who had been taught by the Dominican Thomist Francis Sicuro of Nardò, and Pomponazzi's life-long rival, Agostino Nifo, paid respectful attention to the writings of Aquinas.[25] "Evidently," observes Kristeller, "we cannot expect to discover in them any tendency toward an 'orthodox'

24. *Galileo and His Sources: The Heritage of the Collegio Romano in Galileo's Science* (Princeton, N.J.: Princeton University Press, 1984).

25. Edward P. Mahoney, "Saint Thomas and the School of Padua at the End of the Fifteenth Century," *Proceedings of the American Catholic Philosophical Association* 48 (1974): 277–85.

Thomism as that of the Dominican school, since these philosophers ordinarily did not concern themselves with theological questions and since, in the properly philosophical area, Saint Thomas was simply one of many commentators on Aristotle."[26]

The currents that guided the intellectual life of Europe at the beginning of the sixteenth century were swift and strong, and it must be noted that not every humanist maintained a composed and irenic attitude toward the medieval scholastics, including Saint Thomas. By 1509, the same year that Crockaert began lecturing on the *Summa* in Paris, Erasmus' *Praise of Folly* had already established the exemplar and the tone for expressing the standard grievance: "The methods our scholastics pursue only render more subtle these subtlest of subtleties; for you will escape from a labyrinth more quickly than from the tangles of Realists, Nominalists, Thomists, Albertists, Occamists, Scotists—I have not named all, but the chief ones only."[27] And later in his 1515 *Annotationes in Novum Testamentum,* Erasmus extended his critique to include a direct attack on Aquinas himself, whose theology Erasmus disparaged because Saint Thomas, whom he considered an otherwise bright man, suffered the misfortune of having lived during a time when theologians were generally ignorant of Greek and Hebrew.[28]

Erika Rummel argues that the humanist-scholastic rift, which arguably can be said to begin at the end of the fourteenth century with Petrarch, becomes radicalized at the time of the Reformation

26. Kristeller, "Thomism," p. 53.

27. Desiderius Erasmus, *The Praise of Folly,* trans. Hoyt Hopewell Hudson (Princeton, N.J.: Princeton University Press, 1941), p. 79.

28. See MS Basileae, fol. 228 v. In the "Introduction" to *Annotationes in Novvm Testamentvm (Pars Prima),* ed. P. F. Hovingh (Amsterdam: Elsevier, 2000), p. 31, P. F. Hovingh mentions this criticism made by Erasmus.

controversy.[29] The new humanist learning and the issues that it forced theologians to ponder altered in some ways the course of Thomism. The great authors moved away from the more formal style of debate that dominated the earlier exchanges with Scotism and nominalism, and turned instead to more free-flowing discussion on topics such as the relations of efficacious grace and free will, of divine truthfulness and human intelligence, and of ecclesiastical authority and individual conscience.

The territories lost to Rome in the sixteenth century were no longer hospitable to Roman Catholic theology of any variety, and so Thomism retreated to the Catholic countries, especially those that remained under the political dominion of the Habsburg princes. The results, however, were not disappointing. Between 1497 and 1499, a twenty-nine-year-old Dominican from Gaeta in Italy lectured on the *Summa* at the University of Pavia. Trained in the intellectual milieu of Padua, Thomas de Vio (d. 1534), called Cajetanus after his birthplace, had read Capreolus and so was informed about the history of Thomism and its opponents from 1270 to 1420. Cajetan's own commentaries on Aquinas's works, especially on the *Summa theologiae* first published at Lyons in 1540–41, helped to ensure that Thomism would remain an active power throughout the tumultuous period of the Protestant reform. Jared Wicks has established the important role that Cardinal Cajetan, who served as the Pope's official ambassador to Germany, played in responding to the claims advanced by Luther,[30] and so

29. *The Humanist-Scholastic Debate in the Renaissance and Reformation* (Cambridge: Harvard University Press, 1995).

30. "Thomism between Renaissance and Reformation: The Case of Cajetan," *Archiv für Reformationsgeschichte* 68 (1977): 9–31.

Wicks illustrates the organic relationship that unites Cajetan with those later Thomist divines who served as theological consultants during the Council of Trent. However, Cajetan's own place in the history of Thomism is above all secured by the fact that his commentary on the *Summa theologiae* enjoys quasi-official status by reason of its being included in the critical edition of the *Summa theologiae* commissioned by Pope Leo XIII. His solicitude as a curial cardinal, his commentaries on the Sacred Scriptures, and his leadership as Master of the Dominican Order further contributed to his renown, and indeed merit Cajetan a place among the most significant Thomists of the period.

The work of John Capreolus, *The Books of Arguments in Defense of the Theology of Saint Thomas Aquinas,* continued to exercise influence on the development of Thomist theology after the death of its author in 1444. For example in 1518, one of the first Roman theologians to respond to the complaints raised by Martin Luther was the Dominican Sylvester Mazolinus da Prierio, who had already published in 1497 a *Compendium* of Capreolus's Thomist theology. Later in 1521–22, another handbook based on Capreolus's works appeared under the joint authorship of Paul Barbo da Soncino (d. 1495) and Isidore degli Isolani (d. 1528). The existence of these manuals of theology indicate that by the time of the Protestant Reform there already existed a substantial body of theological literature within the Thomist tradition that served to instruct those charged with preserving the truth of the Catholic faith. Another example of Thomist theology comes from the pen of Francis Silvestri of Ferrara, who was elected Master of the Dominicans in 1525, after he had produced the classical commentary on the *Summa contra gentiles,* which like that of Cajetan on the *Summa* would find its way into the modern Leonine edition. And there were other learned Thomists—Kennedy counts more than 75 Italian Dominican Thomists alone—whose teaching and published works witness to the strength that Thomist theology had attained during the sixteenth century.

During the fifteenth and sixteenth centuries, Thomist theology earned a reputation for benchmark excellence. Fidelity to the whole of revealed truth is what distinguishes good theology from its counterfeits, and other practitioners besides Thomists met this criterion. Still, it is possible to identify certain emphases that marked the theological exercises undertaken by Thomists of this period. Worthy of particular note is the way that they put theology's pieces together so as to exhibit the inner intelligibility of the Christian faith. Although this emphasis on the unity of theology and other themes emerged from reading the texts of Aquinas, the presentation of Aquinas's themes took on new forms in the course of the late medieval debates (which Capreolus chronicled in his *Defensiones*). It was during the course of these exchanges that Thomist theologians sharpened many of their distinctions and further clarified their positions.

The following stances capture the most significant themes that distinguish Thomist theology in its classical expression from other recognized schools of Catholic theology. Thomists affirm that beyond the order of nature there exists a higher, supernatural order of reality, which only God can reveal to the human race and which we in turn embrace through the theological virtue of faith. Thomists further claim that the distinction between grace and nature is not only a modal one *(quoad modum),* but extends also to the very substance of things *(quoad substantiam),* so that without the free gift offered in Christ, one human being or all human beings together can neither strive toward nor attain to beatific fellowship with the blessed Trinity. Faith and grace create in the human person a real participation in God's own truth and life without causing violence to human nature. This is possible because there is a divinely ordered harmony between nature and grace—a harmony which is rooted in the divine constitution of human nature such that it is elevable to divine friendship. (It is also possible because only the One who is the cause of a nature and its natural motion may move it without violence, whether naturally or supernaturally.) Human nature itself is thus with divine aid perfectable along a higher trajectory than that of mere nature, but it is not simply in itself and apart from grace directly ordered to supernatural beatitude. The natural desire for God as cause of the terrestrial cosmos is elevable by grace to become the desire for God as he is in himself and as he abides in supernatural mystery—the supernatural desire for God as Father, Son, and Holy Spirit. No contradiction can arise between what is held in faith and what is known by reason. Still, the fully theological character of the virtue of faith means that no human argument is sufficient to move a person to confess the articles of the Christian creed, since the truthfulness of the divine mysteries which the articles express can find their verification only in God, First Truth, alone. Thomists deeply appreciate that there are certain preambles to Christian faith that reason can demonstrate, but they also are inclined to agree that this kind of reasoning persuades only a few people.

In the area of Christian anthropology, Thomists hold that the human person acts both as a true secondary cause and as a free agent, since the universal causality of God always respects the nature that He has created, even when that nature enjoys the capacity to act freely. The Thomist view on predestination emphasizes with unwavering persistence the primacy of the divine omnipotence and mercy, asserting that God's free choice explains the predestination of certain persons to grace and glory. At the same time, to interpret such a claim as implying that God is whimsical or heartless finds no support in Aquinas or the Thomist tradition, which never ceases to emphasize the superabundant goodness of the all-good God. Thomists, therefore, do not appeal to a divine foreknowledge of how man will react to grace, even when it is proposed that this stratagem can be embellished by postulating a divine middle knowledge *(scientia media)*. Indeed, Thomists consider explanations that require putting human cooperation on the same level with divine power opposed to the first Thomist principle of predestination: God loves us because He is good, not because we are.

Because Thomists stress the superabundance of the divine goodness, they look for no motive cause to explain why God became man other than the need of the human race for a redemptive Incarnation, and they consequently suppose with Aquinas that had there been no sin, there would have been no Incarnation. Furthermore, the logic of the Incarnation extends to the sacraments of the Christian religion which both are expressed in sign-actions and serve as true causes of grace. As instrumental causes, the sacraments effect what they signify *ex opere operato* (see *Summa theologiae* IIIa, q. 62, a. 5). Thomists tend first to think about the Church as a spiritual reality, one that is constituted by the capital grace of Christ—Aquinas's expression for the Pauline notion of Headship—and so are reluctant to consider ecclesiology as an isolated theological topic, one that can be fully explicated apart from full consideration of the grace of Christ. Finally, Thomists hold that eternal life consists in seeing God face to face, and that this *visio* accounts for the superabundant happiness that accompanies perfect communion with God.

The Reformation occasioned fresh expositions of Thomist theology such as the highly popular and thoroughly Catholic works of Pierre Doré (1497–1569). The number of editions of Doré's French works was surpassed only by the same of John Calvin.[31] In some isolated cases, however, Thomist authors bent too much toward accommodating Luther's complaints. Chrysostom Javelli (fl. 1538), for instance, wrote a commentary on the *Summa* that included a special question on predestination and reprobation; the author so aimed to appease Luther, that he departed from the teaching of Thomas Aquinas on merit, as expressed in the traditional thesis of the Thomist school. The work of Javelli reveals that the attempt of Martin Luther to reform the Church prompted many authors to give new interpretations, and sometimes even novel formulation, to the classical theses of Thomist theology, which by the time of the sixteenth-century controversies had been extensively debated throughout the late medieval period. This meant that efforts to reformulate Thomism could always be judged by appeal to Aquinas's own writings and to the common themes of the established commentatorial tradition. At the beginning of the sixteenth century, Thomism had begun in fact to take its position as the Church's official theology, and with that to take on the liabilities that such an honor portends. "Can we be surprised," asks Aegidius Doolan, "that the enemies of the Catholic Faith should have turned away,

31. See John Langlois, *A Catholic Response in Sixteenth-Century France to Reformation Theology—The Works of Pierre Doré,* Roman Catholic Studies, vol. 18 (Lewiston, N.Y.: The Edwin Mellen Press, 2003).

almost angrily, from the doctrines of St. Thomas? Luther confessed himself more than doubtful about Saint Thomas's salvation, and referred to his followers as 'Thomistic hogs.'"[32]

Many Dominicans were active at the Council of Trent (1545–63); not all of them can be numbered among true Thomists, a most obvious example being Bishop Ambrose Catharinus (d. 1553), who defended the Immaculate Conception and other non-Thomistic positions. But the majority of theologians at the Council followed the mind and spirit of Thomas Aquinas. The Italian polemicist Bartholomew Spina (d. 1546), who considered Catharinus a heretic, and the Spanish jurist Dominic de Soto (d. 1560) were among those who helped during the first sessions (1545–48). At the university, De Soto wrote on the nature of law and against Pelagianism, besides helping Bartholomew de las Casas defend the full human status of the native American peoples. During the second period of the Council of Trent (1551–52), conflict emerged between the distinguished Salamancan theologian Melchior Cano (d. 1569) and the Dominican archbishop of Toledo, Bartholomew de Carranza (d. 1576), who as a result suffered a lengthy confinement in Rome on the charge that his *Catechism* expressed Protestant sympathies.[33] In his *De locis theologicis,* Cano was the first theologian, Thomist or otherwise, to address the nature of theological argument and to attempt a classification of the sources of theology. During the third period of the Council (1562–63), Thomist commentators on the *Summa theologiae* like the Italian bishop Bartholomew of the Martyrs (d. 1590), and the Spaniard John Gallo

32. *The Revival of Thomism* (Dublin: Clonmore & Reynolds, 1951), p. 23.

33. The successor to Pope Saint Pius V, Pope Gregory XIII nonetheless ordered the following epitaph for the archbishop's tomb: "Viro genere, vita, doctrina, contione atque elemosinis claro."

(d. 1575), who wrote a full-length commentary on the *Sentences,* brought to completion the drafting of schemas that the Thomists had undertaken throughout the period of the Council.

The achievement of Thomist authors at the Council of Trent is expressed not only in their influence on the decrees of the Council, especially those on justification, on the sacraments in general, and on the Eucharist in particular, but also in their work on the *Roman Catechism* that was published by the Dominican Pope Pius V in 1566. The Catholic Reform marked a new moment in the history of Thomism, and even the new orders that were founded during the period after Trent adopted Aquinas as their teacher and safeguard of sound teaching. Thomism itself quickly became identified with Catholic orthodoxy to such an extent that a popular but erroneous rumor circulated to the effect that the Fathers of the Council had enshrined the *Summa* of Saint Thomas Aquinas on the altar next to the Bible. What is true, however, is that, on 11 April 1567, Pius V gave official sanction to the directions of Thomist theology by taking the innovative step of officially ranking Thomas Aquinas among the four recognized Doctors of the Church.[34] In 1588, a later Pope accorded the same honors to Saint Bonaventure, but the pull of gravity toward Aquinas was so strong that when Peter Trigoso de Calatayud, a Jesuit who had switched to the Capuchin Order, published his *Sancti Bonaventurae Summa Theologica* in 1593, to some degree he likened Bonaventure to Thomas Aquinas.

Dominic Báñez (d. 1604), who inherited the rich tradition of Thomist theology that began with Francisco de Vitoria and continued in Melchior Cano and Dominic de Soto, represents the many

34. For further information, see Nicole Lemaitre, *Saint Pie V* (Paris: Fayard, 1994), p. 168.

illustrious Thomists who guided the Catholic Reform in Spain. Báñez held several professorships in other Spanish universities before returning to Salamanca in 1577 where he acquired a reputation for great learning. At the peak of his career, Báñez's influence was felt in almost every position of importance in Spain, and he numbered among those who sought his counsel both the Habsburg emperor Philip II and the great Carmelite reformer Teresa of Avila.

Báñez symbolizes the flourishing of a new strain in Thomist theology, one that picks up on the themes found in late-medieval German mysticism, but without the deviations that stemmed from its over-reliance on Neoplatonism. The practice of the Spanish Thomists of composing special commentaries on the gifts of the Holy Spirit, oftentimes as part of their *Summa* notes, illustrates this renewed interest in the interior life. Báñez himself produced a sample of this genre in his 1584 *In secundum secundae*, q. 8 (ed. Bernardum Iuntam, Venice, 1586), but the Portuguese-born Dominican John Poinsot (d. 1644) best exemplifies the Thomist propensity for combining affective theology with brilliant philosophical analysis. His treatise *De donis Spiritus Sancti*[35] remains to the present day a classic of Christian spirituality, and has been translated into several modern languages, which distinguishes this small treatise on the spiritual life from many other pieces of Thomist commentary that remain in their original languages, mostly Latin.

A seventeenth-century professor of theology at Alcalá de Henares, John of St. Thomas, as Poinsot is also known, epitomizes Spanish scholasticism at the end of the *siglo de oro*. He began his teaching career at about the same time that El Greco died. This

---

35. *Cursus theologicus. In Summam Theologicam D. Thomae.* I-II, Disputatio XVIII in the Vivès edition, vol. VI (Paris, 1885).

Iberian scholastic stands in the lineage of the late medieval and renaissance commentators on Aquinas, and though a near contemporary of Descartes, he pointed in directions quite different from those intuitions that inaugurated "la pensée moderne." The Discalced Carmelite theologians at Salamanca, known as the "Salmanticenses," recognized the merits in John of St. Thomas's theological abilities;[36] at the same time, their own voluminous writings on the *Summa* fill twenty volumes in the Paris edition of 1870–73. John of St. Thomas is also esteemed for his *Cursus philosophicus thomisticus,* which was used to teach logic and natural philosophy in seminary training programs until the mid-twentieth century, though sometimes in the digested form of Josef Gredt's *Elementa Philosophiae.*

John of St. Thomas does not stand in isolation, but is one of a large number of Thomists who contributed to the reform and revival of Christian theology in seventeenth-century Spain and elsewhere. These Thomists, mostly Dominicans, worked side by side the Jesuit scholastics who shared their interest in, but not always their interpretation of, the texts of Aquinas. The founder of the Jesuits, St. Ignatius of Loyola (d. 1556), had been trained by the Dominicans, and the first Jesuit professors were Thomists in philosophy and theology. But from its inception, the Society of Jesus leaned toward promoting a correlational approach, which St. Ignatius himself warmly recommended as a new work "more accommodated to our times." By the end of the sixteenth century, Jesuit scholastics such as Luis de Molina, Gabriel Vázquez, and especially the influential Francisco Suárez were developing forms of eclectic Thomism that would provide the groundwork for the *intrascholam* debates of the seventeenth and eighteenth centuries.

36. See their *Cursus theologiae, De spe,* Disp. 4, dub. 4, n. 43.

In the case of Suárez, the designation "eclectic" should not detract from his standing as a highly original thinker, especially in the areas of philosophy of law and metaphysics. Still, Suárez consciously develops and espouses non-Thomist positions on a series of key philosophical and theological issues. Some significant examples include: (1) the distinction between essence and existence, which Suárez held to have its origin in the mind, inasmuch as making distinctions of this kind are one of the things that the human mind does and which he denied as being in any sense real; (2) the problem of individuation, or the way to explain how many individuals participate in one universal essence, which Suárez, revealing a characteristically modern preference for the empirical, argued can be adequately explained simply by appeal to the brute fact that a given form unites with matter; (3) the reconciliation of genuine human freedom with divine omnipotence, which Suárez describes in terms of a divine and human interaction, conceived after the fashion of the cooperation that two created agents undertake as much as each of them contributes partially to the production of a given effect. Suárez, like Molina, rejects the Thomist view that God's physical pre-actuation *(praemotio physica)* can shape free human actions, and instead posits a congruism of divine work and human effort that accents the latter element in the grace efficacious for performing a salutary act. Suárez also departs from Thomist teaching on the nature of law, as realized in eternal, natural, divine, and human law. Specifically, he rejects the position that law embodies an ordinance of reason, and insists instead that all law, given its purpose in human society, results only from the legislator's will to obligate and therein finds its defining reality. On Suárez's account, Aquinas's opinion that law is expressive of the divine reason may say something about the reality of law in the receptive subject, but does not define what constitutes law as an effective agent of sovereignty. Suárez's view on human freedom correlates with his view of law. He defines human liberty as an "active indifference" waiting, as it were, to be obliged.

Controversies inevitably developed. The most renowned involved the *Congregatio de Auxiliis* (1598–1607), which refers to an officially monitored debate between Jesuit and Dominican theologians on the question on the efficacy of grace in the free will of man and God's foreknowledge of man's free actions. The theological claims of the Protestant Reformers, especially the unbending views of John Calvin, made such questions almost inevitable ones for Catholic theologians to face, but the results were not always satisfying. The Jesuits in fact argued that the Dominican position was indistinguishable from that of Calvin, whereas the Dominicans retorted that the Jesuits had reintroduced Pelagianism into the Christian life. Even after years of patient debate and commission work, no authoritative declarations were delivered by the Holy See, which instead preferred to counsel forbearance to both parties. Although today many believe that these debates served only to expose the Achilles' heel in the scholastic method of theological argument, others consider that the failure to resolve the questions raised in the *De auxiliis* debates resulted in the *de facto* separation of the moral life from the world of divine grace, infused virtues, and gifts of the Holy Spirit.

Shortly after the start of the Catholic reform, moral theology developed into a science of religious jurisprudence. Servais Pinckaers has clearly shown that the rise of casuistry as a new form of moral theology constituted a complete departure from the doctrine of Saint Thomas Aquinas.[37] The Spanish Dominican Bartolomé de Medina (d. 1581) developed a maneuver called "probabilism" to deal with the casuist method in morals, but it soon became clear that the probabilist position could degenerate quickly into moral laxism, and so the Dominican Order officially banned it in 1656. Conflicts between Jansenists and the Jesuits, who in the meantime had made probabilism their own, produced much conflict for more than two centuries. In the end, the field was dominated by St. Alphonsus Liguori, whose *Theologia moralis* (1753–55) aimed to provide practical guidance for Christian consciences, while trying to avoid as much as possible the subtleties and even sophistries of many casuist disputes. Still, casuistry retained hegemony in the Church until the Second Vatican Council, which, by its call for the renewal of moral theology, once again invited interest in the distinctive features of moral theology found in the *secunda pars* of Aquinas's *Summa theologiae*.[38]

The debates with the Jesuits over the doctrine of grace and with those who advanced the cause of probabilism dominated the intellectual activity of Thomists right up until the moment of the French Revolution. But Thomists also continued to develop a general theological culture in which the thought of Aquinas was analyzed and brought into dialogue with contemporary learning. During the seventeenth century, France alone produced a large number of Thomist authors, such as Jean-Baptiste Gonet (d. 1681), author

37. See his *The Sources of Christian Ethics,* trans. Sr. Mary Thomas Noble, O.P. (Washington, D.C.: The Catholic University of America Press, 1995).

38. For further information, see my *The Moral Virtues and Theological Ethics* (Notre Dame, Ind.: University of Notre Dame Press, 1991) and my *Virtues, or the Examined Life* (New York: Continuum, 2002).

of the *Clypeus theologiae thomisticae,* and Alexander Piny (d. 1709), author of *Quaestiones inter Thomistas et Molinistas.* In addition, commentaries on the *Summa theologiae* were produced by theologians of every nationality and included a large number of tomes written in the New World. Not only Catholics consulted Aquinas, but it has been shown that his works were known and widely used throughout the seventeenth century also by English Protestant writers, including King James I. However, since many of these commentaries, compendia, and courses have not been fully examined, it is difficult to determine to what degree the Catholic authors represent strict or eclectic Thomism. What is perhaps of greater significance is that interest in the texts of Aquinas reached as far as China, where two translations of the *Summa theologiae* into Chinese were published by Jesuit missionaries in Peking between 1654 and 1678. Given the positivist mood that dominated theological procedures in the last quarter of the twentieth century, it is difficult to appreciate the richness of theological culture that these Thomist commentaries and textbooks represent, and so a proper judgment on their merits must await a time when a stronger consensus exists among theologians on the character of theology as a sapiential discipline.

The commentatorial tradition was carried on into the eighteenth century by authors such as the Dominican Noël Alexander (d. 1724), an enormously erudite controversialist who published his *Summa S. Thomae vindicata* in 1675 at Paris, and the Belgian Charles René Billuart (d. 1757), who published his *Le thomisme vengé* at Brussels in 1720, though his major work consisted in a nineteen-volume commentary on the whole of the *Summa theologiae* that drew considerably on the earlier commentary of the Italian Cardinal Vincent Louis Gotti (d. 1742). Lesser-known figures contributed their compositions to the large pool of Thomist literature that continued to develop in the eighteenth century. However, Daniel Concina (d. 1756) should not be placed among the obscure authors, since his multi-volume works in moral theology, based on Aquinas's *prima-secundae,* aimed to reintroduce a teleological approach to the moral life and emphasized charity as the means for finding union with God.

From about 1789 to 1850 religious houses in France, Belgium, Germany, and even many in Italy were suppressed. It comes, therefore, as no surprise that the second half of the eighteenth century was not a particularly fruitful period for their school. Thomism however did not disappear.[39] The eighth printing of the complete works of Aquinas was accomplished at Venice between 1745 and 1788, the second such printing to have occurred in that city. Moreover, among the many works that Thomists produced during the first half of the eighteenth century, two volumes especially are worthy of note: *Theologica scholastica* by Hilarion Negrebetskii and *Scientia sacra* by Teofilatto Loptinskii. These were published in Czarist Russia during the 1730s, and they illustrate the universality that Thomism had achieved under the *ancien regime.*

39. See Philippe Lécrivain, "La *Somme théologique* de Thomas d'Aquin aux 16ᵉ–18ᵉ siècles," *Recherches de Science Religieuse* 91 (2003): 397–427.

Chapter Three

AFTER THE FRENCH REVOLUTION

Though the Church and her institutions suffered at the hands of the French Revolutionaries as well as from the social reforms that Napoleon and his proxies introduced into most of Europe, these and other civil disturbances did not succeed in eradicating the Thomist tradition. The texts of Thomas Aquinas, in one form or another, still were available and transmitted. In fact, new historical research has uncovered evidence of the sustained interest in Thomism that flourished, especially among Italian ecclesiastics, through the late eighteenth and into the early nineteenth centuries.[1] The Kennedy *Catalogue* lists more than three hundred Thomists at work during the nineteenth century in Italy alone. The political upheavals of this period affected religious orders more than the diocesan clergy, and so the vast majority of

---

1. For example, see *Saggi sulla rinascita del Tomismo nel secolo XIX* (Città del Vaticano: Libreria Editrice Vaticana, 1974).

these Thomists belonged to groups other than the old religious institutes. At the same time, as they began to recover from one form of suppression or another, Dominicans, certain Jesuits, and also the Vincentians, who were instituted to train the diocesan clergy, found themselves in positions to cultivate the continuance of Thomism.

The intellectual tradition of Thomism took on new prominence at the Alberoni College conducted by the Vincentian Fathers at Piacenza in Northern Italy.[2] One figure who symbolizes the continuity between the Thomism practiced under the *ancien regime* and what customarily has been called Neo-Thomism is the Italian Jesuit Serafino Sordi (d. 1865), who was born at Piacenza in 1793. By the end of the first quarter of the nineteenth century, Sordi, who at Piacenza had been a pupil of *maestro* Vincenzo Buzzetti (d. 1824), was giving instruction in logic, metaphysics, and ethics. Sordi belonged to a circle of teachers who came to recognize the value of Thomism for refuting those philosophical positions that, since they exemplified for the most part either a developed Kantianism or an accommodated Hegelianism, proved ill-suited to elucidate Christian theology. The publication of *Aeterni Patris* can be considered as one of the achievements of this group. It should be noted that the manuals of philosophy that Sordi wrote were still in use into the mid-twentieth century: *Ontologia* (Milan, 1940) and *Theologia naturalis* (Milan, 1945).

Even in the late seventeenth century, in order mainly to meet the pedagogical requirements of students preparing for the minis-

2. Giovanni Felice Rossi, *Il movimento neotomista piacentino iniziato al Collegio Alberoni da Franceasco Grassi nel 1751 e la formazione di Vincenzo Buzzetti* (Città del Vaticano: Libreria Editrice Vaticana, 1974).

terial priesthood, manuals of philosophy began to replace Aquinas's commentaries on Aristotle and other of his philosophical works. One of the earliest and most influential examples of the genre came from the pen of the French Dominican Antoine Goudin (d. 1695), whose *Philosophia Juxta D. Thomae Dogmata* had gone through fourteen editions by 1744. And after Dominican Master John Thomas Boxadors recommitted the Dominican Order to the study of Aquinas in 1757, the Neapolitan Dominican Salvatore Roselli (d. 1784) produced his six-volume series, *Summa philosophiae ad mentem Angelici Doctoris Thomae Aquinatis,* which by 1777 had been published in Rome. Some intellectual historians have criticized the manual tradition on the basis that it replaced critical engagement in philosophical dialogue, such as that practiced by Aquinas and his first disciples, with a synthesized presentation of principles and conclusions. While this critique remains persuasive for some, the fact remains that Canon Buzzetti, who began his intellectual life as a disciple of John Locke, learned his Thomism and became convinced of its value by reading the manuals of Goudin and Roselli. His personal experience illustrates that the Thomist manuals could serve to open up to well-disposed persons an alternative vision of philosophy. Vincenzo Buzzetti came to recognize that the modern period had not produced the kind of philosophical guidance for Catholic theologians that would keep Catholic theology from tumbling into eclecticism.

Scholars like Serafino Sordi and others, such as Carlo Maria Curci (d. 1891) and Giovanni Maria Cornoldi (d. 1892), carried on a tradition of Thomist learning, particularly in philosophy, that flourished among some intelligent clerics in the Italian region of Emilia-Romagna. Many of these men joined the Jesuits after the

Society was restored in 1814 and then tried to persuade their fellow Jesuits that the wisdom of Thomas Aquinas could serve as a trustworthy guide for renewing Catholic philosophy and theology. Gerald McCool reports, however, that their attempts to convince other members of the Society to return to the thought of Aquinas met with only mixed results.[3] The Roman Jesuits put up the first resistance. After the Collegio Romano, today known as the Gregorian University, had again been committed to the auspices of the Jesuits in 1824, Luigi Taparelli d'Azeglio made a concerted effort to guarantee unity and coherence in the philosophy program by encouraging the faculty to study the doctrine of Aquinas. Only a few Jesuits were amenable to the proposal, and these were reduced to studying hand-written notes that had been put together by Serafino Sordi.

In the short term, the initial effort at Rome to spark interest in the thought of Aquinas failed, as did a later attempt among the Jesuits in Naples, despite the aid of Domenico Sordi, a blood brother of Serafino. Though while in Rome, Taparelli d'Azeglio did succeed in influencing the young Gioacchino Pecci, who in 1828 was prompted to send home for a copy of the *Summa theologiae* that he remembered seeing on the shelves of his family library. By the time Pecci was elected Pope in 1878, Thomism had already enjoyed a half century of renewal. So as one of his first administrative actions, Leo XIII was able to replace the Cartesian philosophy textbooks then being used in the Roman seminary with respected manuals of Thomism, including the *Summa Philosophica* of his longtime friend Tommaso Zigliara (d. 1893). Until his death, the

---

3. *The Neo-Thomists* (Milwaukee: Marquette University Press, 1994).

Dominican Zigliara remained a papal counselor to Leo, and he was instrumental in establishing the Leonine Commission to produce a critical edition of all of the works of Thomas Aquinas. The Commission continues in session and trains new recruits to carry on its work.

A change of direction within the Society of Jesus had already occurred by 1853, when the Jesuit Matteo Liberatore, who had been a student under Taparelli in Naples, turned the journal *Civiltà Cattolica* into a vehicle for advertising the usefulness of Thomism. As it happened, Naples had conserved a strong Thomist tradition among the Dominicans, whose influence accounts for the existence of so many nineteenth-century Thomists of Neapolitan origin. One of these was the secular priest Gaetano Sansaverino (d. 1865), whose contributions to the development of Thomist thought, in addition to numerous publications, included the foundation of the first academy of Thomist philosophy in Italy. The texts redacted by Zigliara and Sansaverino played a prominent role in the education of clergy and also influenced others active in developing modern Catholic thought. In Spain, the Dominican Zephirino González y Diaz Tuñon (d. 1894), later cardinal-archbishop of Toledo, was instrumental in bringing about a similar state of affairs. He introduced textbooks into the seminaries that incorporated philosophy inspired by the writings of Aquinas.

The German Jesuit Josef Kleutgen, whose five volumes, *Die Theologie der Vorzeit,* were published between 1853 and 1870, had already been working in Rome since 1843. These five volumes, writes McCool, "mounted a persuasive argument in favor of Kleutgen's thesis that the nineteenth century Catholic theologies, whose philosophical framework had been taken over from the philosophical systems of the modern age *(Neuzeit)* were not as well equipped to expound and defend the Catholic faith as the older Scholastic theology employed by the Church in pre-Enlightenment times *(Vorzeit)*."[4] Kleutgen's view directed the efforts of Thomists in the period after 1879, although no general agreement emerged as to how the basic doctrines of Thomas Aquinas can best serve the Church's needs in the modern period. On the other hand, Kleutgen's studies of Aquinas did exercise an influence on the deliberations of Vatican Council I (1869–70). He was summoned by the deputation on faith to revise the first *schema* for the constitution *De fide catholica,* which, though mainly the work of his fellow Jesuit and prominent theologian Johannes Franzelin, had not been favorably received by the conciliar fathers. Just as Thomism significantly influenced the formulation of Trent's decrees, the short constitution of Vatican I on the Catholic faith, *Dei Filius,* reflects Thomist views on faith and reason. While the definition of papal infallibility is not alien to Thomist theology, this grace of the Petrine office remains more assumed than articulated in the teachings of Aquinas.

Some authors continued the tradition of eclectic Thomism. A little more than a half century after *Aeterni Patris,* the Jesuit Karl Rahner, who would become one of the most influential theologians in the post-concilar period, was ready to publish his *Spirit in the World (Geist im Welt)*. This work marks a milestone in the project of Transcendental Thomism. In general terms, the Transcendental Thomist proceeds on the assumption that the critical turn introduced into Western thought by Immanuel Kant has rendered

4. McCool, *Neo-Thomists,* pp. 31–32.

obsolete the theory of knowledge that Aquinas took from Aristotle, and so argues that the only way to gain a hearing in the world of contemporary philosophy is to follow the path blazed by thinkers such as the Belgian Jesuit Joseph Maréchal and continued, among others, by the Canadian Jesuit Bernard J. F. Lonergan. Transcendental Thomism enjoyed its greatest popularity among theologians who worked in the period after the Second Vatican Council (1962–65), but the publication of the *Catechism of the Catholic Church* in 1992 reveals that their exercises and formulations did not alter the way that the Church authentically expresses the Catholic faith. In other words, there is much evidence to suggest that Kleutgen's basic insight still holds true.

No discussion of twentieth-century Thomism can fail to mention two illustrious lay Thomists, Jacques Maritain (d. 1973) and Étienne Gilson (d. 1979). Although both native Frenchmen, their influences have been especially felt in North America. Gilson founded the Pontifical Institute for Mediaeval Studies in Toronto, which continued his serious investigation into the historical background of Aquinas's thought, and Maritain taught many years in the United States, including for a period at the University of Notre Dame, which still houses a center dedicated to promoting his work. Maritain influenced American philosophy, especially, in the fields of aesthetics and political philosophy. Both Maritain and Gilson made significant contributions in the general area of Thomist methodology, although Maritain's 1932 *Three Degrees of Knowledge* and Gilson's 1949 *Being and Some Philosophers* reveal differences between the philosophical frames of mind of each of these eminent Thomists. Maritain carried on an extensive correspondence with the Swiss abbé and later cardinal Charles Journet, whose many books helped popularize the theological perspectives of Thomism.

Interest in the historical background of Aquinas and of Thomism captured some of the brightest theological minds of the twentieth century, many of them associated with the *studium* of the Paris Dominicans. (Since 1903 this studium has been known as Le Saulchoir, a name that derives from the region in Belgium where, for reasons of French politics, the Dominicans set up their house of studies before returning definitively to France in 1937.) Pierre Mandonnet devoted himself to historical studies that illumined the medieval context in which Aquinas lived and worked, whereas the celebrated M.-D. Chenu recalled the methodological place that history holds in theology. As early as 1937, Father Chenu expressed some of his views about history and theology in a small work, *Une École de théologie: Le Saulchoir*;[5] it was poorly received in Rome and subsequently led to the author's temporary removal from Le Saulchoir. The Parisian approach to reading Aquinas, well captured in Father Chenu's brief but tightly argued essay *Saint Thomas d'Aquin et la théologie*,[6] eventually bore fruit for the renewal of theology, especially in the work of Cardinal Y.-M. Congar, whose studies on the laity, like those of his Belgian confrère Cardinal Jerome Hamer on the nature of the Church, greatly influenced the bishops of the Second Vatican Council.

Thomist theologians enjoyed a period of special influence during the middle decades of the twentieth century. One of the best known is the French Dominican Réginald Garrigou-Lagrange (d.

5. Paris: Les Éditions du Cerf, 1985, with commentaries by Giuseppe Alberigo and other authors.

6. Paris: Editions du Seuil, 1963.

1964), whose highly structured and illuminating presentation of Roman Catholic theology influenced generations of students both before and after the Second World War at the Pontifical University of Saint Thomas in Rome. But there is also the Provençale Dominican Jean-Hervé Nicolas, sometime professor of theology at the University of Fribourg, whose two-volume *Synthèse dogmatique*[7] illustrates the benefits that accrue from employing a unified method in theology. Earlier at Fribourg, this typically Thomist achievement was modeled by the Spaniard Santiago Ramírez (d. 1967), who produced penetrating commentaries on Aquinas's texts, especially the *prima secundae*. In Toulouse, French Dominican Marie-Michel Labourdette contributed important essays to the *Revue Thomiste* and by his classroom lectures and notes reminded several generations of students of the distinctive features that distinguish Thomist moral theology.[8]

European scholars have contributed much to ensuring that Thomism remained a viable intellectual tradition in the twentieth century, and they have accomplished this to a large extent by illuminating the profundity of Aquinas's metaphysical insights, especially his appreciation for the act of existence. Two disciples of Maréchal, Joseph de Finance and André Hayen, published works on this theme around the time of the Second World War. And the Alsatian Dominican philosopher, Louis-Bertrand Geiger even called attention to the "awkwardness" of *esse* in his ground-breaking *La participation dans la philosophie de S. Thomas d'Aquin*.[9]

7. Paris: Editions Beauchesne, 1985 & 1993.
8. For further information, see the issue of the *Revue Thomiste* (Janvier–Mars 1992) dedicated to this "maître en théologie."
9. Paris: Vrin, 1942.

Other students of Aquinas, such as the Dominicans who constituted the Albertus Magnus Lyceum in Chicago, observed that too exclusive a concentration on metaphysical themes risks eclipsing the decidedly empiricist cast that Aquinas's philosophy took over from Aristotle. Instead they proposed a reading of Aquinas that, while it recognizes metaphysics as "first" in the order of reflection, places the study of being-that-becomes or natural science first in the order of learning.[10] Thomists influenced by the River Forest School of Theology, which takes its name from the suburb of Chicago where these scholars met and worked, have been able to demonstrate the relevance of Aquinas's thought in different arenas of scientific enquiry.[11]

The scope of Thomism since the beginning of the twentieth century can be gleaned from a study of the *Bulletin thomiste,* published at Le Saulchoir, near Paris, and its successor, the *Rassegna di letteratura tomistica,* published in Naples. While articles on the thought of Aquinas appear in every sort of scientific journal, several reviews are especially dedicated to the advancement of Thomism, including the *Revue thomiste,* edited under the auspices of the Dominican faculty in Toulouse, and *The Thomist,* published at Washington, D.C. In addition, there exists a comprehensive survey of materials that demonstrate the vitality of Thomism: *Thomistic Bibliography, 1940–1978,*[12] compiled by Terry L. Miethe and Vernon

10. For further information, see Benedict M. Ashley, "The River Forest School and the Philosophy of Nature Today," in *Philosophy and the God of Abraham,* ed. R. James Long (Toronto: Pontifical Institute of Mediaeval Studies, 1991).

11. William A. Wallace, *The Modeling of Nature. Philosophy of Science and Philosophy of Nature in Synthesis* (Washington, D.C.: The Catholic University of America Press, 1996).

12. London: Greenwood Press, 1980.

J. Bourke, and its sequel, *Thomas Aquinas: International Bibliography 1977–1990,* edited by Richard Ingardia.[13] These latter instruments of research, however, make no attempt to distinguish eclectic Thomists from others working in the field.

It is tempting to conclude that Thomism at the end of the twentieth century finds itself in a position not much different from when it began in the thirteenth century. The study of Aquinas continues in the universities: Paris, Oxford, Bologna, Cracow and on around the globe. But if the history of Thomism provides a prologue for its future, then it will not be surprising to witness Aquinas's influence spread to other arenas of ecclesial life, and even contribute to shaping the civilization of love whose foundation remains the one Truth that God has revealed in Jesus Christ. It was to the contemplation of this highest Truth that Aquinas consecrated his every word.

13. Bowling Green, Ohio: The Philosophy Documentation Center, 1993. See also Helen James John, *The Thomist Spectrum* (New York: Fordham University Press, 1966).

CONCLUSION

The preceding pages tell about the many Thomists who have developed the one Thomism. Who are they? Thomists are scholars of all sorts who have inserted themselves into a living tradition of historical, philosophical, and theological reflection that finds its origin and sustaining force in the work of a most eminent Christian figure who lived during the High Middle Ages. Without Thomas Aquinas, of course, there would be no Thomism. But something else is also true: without active Thomists, very little of Thomas Aquinas nowadays would be available to us. The present account of Thomism and its partisans argues that what Thomas Aquinas inaugurates is best understood as a continuum of intellectual achievement, one that begins in the last quarter of the thirteenth century and remains active to the present moment.[1]

1. One of the best and most recent signs of the vitality that springs from Thomism is the inception of an English edition of the international theological journal *Nova et Vetera*. The American editors, Matthew Levering and Michael Dauphinais, collaborate with British and continental Thomists, including a promising young generation of Dominican priests located in Toulouse, Oxford, Rome, and Fribourg.

As an intellectual movement, Thomism owes its existence to the great number of practicing Thomists who have pondered the thought of Aquinas and then interpreted it for the benefit of their audiences, albeit within the various historical contingencies that mark what one might call the doctrinal history of Western Christendom. In the brief space that a study of this kind allows, it has been my intention to stress the real, dare I say the personal, unity that binds all these diverse members of the Thomist school. By examining, even in a brief and cursory way, the work of past and present Thomists, their manuscripts and printed volumes, their translations, commentaries, and compendia, I have endeavored to establish clearly that Thomism is not an abstraction, but an active force that has shaped the minds of clerics as well as of lay and religious scholars in a most personal way. The influence of Thomists has been and is felt not only within the world of ecclesiastical scholarship—although admittedly it is there that Thomism most often has found fertile soil—but also in the broader venues of Western philosophy.

Obviously, an intellectual movement that has lasted for more than seven centuries merits a place among the great traditions of Western thought. One can speak of Thomism in the same breath as Aristotelianism, Platonism (with all of its sub-varieties), and Augustinianism. Of course, to make such a claim also raises the interpretive question of the relationship of a great figure to the tradition that follows him, as well as the rapport that such a tradition enjoys with its own history. The present work proceeds on the assumption that, just as Aquinas cannot be separated from subsequent Thomists, so also Thomism cannot be detached from its own history. As the present editor of the *Revue Thomiste,* Serge-Thomas Bonino, O.P., puts it: "To abstract Saint Thomas—no matter the effort at contextualization—from the tradition that has brought him to us winds up falling definitively into the trap that one had hoped to avoid: that is, to make of St. Thomas a thinker removed from history, and of Thomism a Platonic Idea."[2] The actual interest at this time in taking a close look at the Thomist tradition offers the best evidence that Thomists are determined to keep Aquinas and his school in the flow of things.

To emphasize the unity of the Thomist tradition is not to ignore the fact that significant divergences have developed even among non-eclectic members of the school. Thomists, it must be admitted, have carried on their work differently during the various periods that compose the history of their movement. It also remains the case that Thomism has fared better at certain moments than at others. Without presuming to bring closure to questions that still require further exploration, I have remarked on both the blessings and the adversities that have befallen Thomists during the past seven centuries. One sure blessing for Thomism has been the school spirit that various religious orders, including the one to which Saint Thomas himself belonged, have demonstrated on behalf of the works and perspectives of the Common Doctor. In a real sense, Thomism belongs to the schools. The explicit institutional recognition of the Roman Catholic Church also should be numbered among the fortunes that Thomism has enjoyed, as well as the support that it has received from secular sources, such as universities and funding agencies.

At various junctures in its history, Thomism has suffered peri-

---

2. *Revue Thomiste* 97 (1997): 5–8: "Car, abstraire saint Thomas—aussi contexualisé qu'on le voudra—de la tradition qui l'a véhiculé jusqu'à nous revient en définitive à retomber dans le piège qu'on a voulu éviter: faire de saint Thomas un penseur en surplomb de l'histoire, et du thomisme une Idée platonicienne."

ods of decline and even reversal. The religious conflicts that plagued Europe during the sixteenth century dealt a blow to Catholic education in general, and the secular revolutions of the modern period contributed in turn to frustrating the work of not only Thomists but also other religious scholars. In other, more peaceful times, the development of eclectic varieties of Thomism have pressed Thomists to articulate more clearly the non-gainsayable principles of their school, so as to keep Thomism from becoming too much of an expandable term. Although no official body enjoys the authority to excommunicate someone from the company of Thomists, the fact remains that some starting points in philosophy and theology are incompatible with those of Aquinas. When this principle is not recognized and honored, Thomism is threatened with a certain instability, no matter how intellectually compelling the *soi-disant* brand of Thomism may appear.

It is fair to conclude, I believe, that the fortunes of Thomism by far outstrip its misfortunes, and that the teachings of Thomas Aquinas will continue to serve the task that is incumbent on every Christian thinker, namely, to ponder a truth that comes from somewhere outside the givens of human history and experience, indeed, a truth that comes instead as a gracious gift from a God who made us and to whom we are all destined to return. Thomism, we know, centers the searching mind on God, from whom all blessings flow, and then moves to capture the searcher's heart. The supreme blessing that first drew the attention of Aquinas is the mystery before which he knelt each day, the blessed gift of the hidden Godhead, which under the figures of bread and wine held Aquinas captive to his Lord, and which today continues to sustain those Thomists who want to enter into his thought with the most perfect assurance.

Index of Names, Subjects, and Book Titles

A Short History of Thomism was designed in Adobe Garamond by Kachergis Book Design
of Pittsboro, North Carolina. It was printed on sixty-pound Glatfelter Natural Offset
and bound by McNaughton & Gunn, Inc., Saline, Michigan.